Air War Over Korea

By Jim Mesko
Color by Don Greer
Illustrated by Andrew Probert

D1244828

USSR

China

Yalu River

Chosin Reservoir

Yudam-ni · Hagaru

Koto-ri

Hamhung · Hungnam

Yonpo Airfield

Sea of Japan
(East Sea)

Pyongyang

Kaeseong · Panmunjom

38th
Parallel

A-17
A-9

Munsan-ni

Ascom City (A-33)

Seoul
(K-16)

Kangneung (K-18)

Yellow
Sea

Inchon

Hoengsong
(K-46)

Kimpo (K-14)

Pyontaek (K-6)

Pohang (K-3)

Kunsan (K-8)

Taejeon (K-5)

Pusan   Perimeter,
10-15 September 1950

Taegu (K-2)

Pusan (K-1/K-9)

Chinhae (K-10)

Sachon (K-4)

squadron/signal publications

Captain Manuel 'Pete' Fernandez, flying an F-86F-1-NA Sabre (51-2857), downs a North Korean MiG-15 over 'MiG Alley' during the spring of 1953. This aircraft was also used by Major James Jabara for many of his 'kills.' Both pilots flew for the 334th Fighter Intercept Squadron (FIS), 4th Fighter Intercept Wing (FIW). Fernandez initially led the 'ace race' and ended the Korean war with 14.5 victories – surpassed only by Capt Joseph McConnell's 16 'kills' and Jabara's 15 victories.

Acknowledgements

National Archives, Washington, DC
Bob Ivy
US Air Force
Dana Bell
US Navy
Bob and Jim Dunderdale
US Marine Corps
US Army
John Horne
Australian War Memorial, Canberra
Stephen Sewell

Author's Note:

During the writing of this book, I was given translated material from recently declassified Russian Archives. Some of this material is at odds with the currently accepted official US versions of certain events. Where applicable, this new information has been inserted to provide the reader with both versions in order to allow for future research in these areas. The author does not discredit previous accepted historical accounts, but feels that, as more information becomes available from Soviet Archives through a variety of sources, new light will be shed on the air war over Korea.

ISBN 0-89747-415-5

If you have any photographs of aircraft, armor, soldiers or ships of any nation, particularly wartime snapshots, why not share them with us and help make Squadron/Signal's books all the more interesting and complete in the future. Any photograph sent to us will be copied and the original returned. The donor will be fully credited for any photos used. Please send them to:

Squadron/Signal Publications, Inc.
1115 Crowley Drive
Carrollton, TX 75011-501010

Если у вас есть фотографии самолётов, вооружения, солдат или кораблей любой страны, особенно, снимки времён войны, поделитесь с нами и помогите сделать новые книги издательства Эскадрон/Сигнал ещё интереснее. Мы переснимем ваши фотографии и вернем оригиналы. Имена приславших снимки будут сопровождать все опубликованные фотографии. Пожалуйста, присылайте фотографии по адресу:

Squadron/Signal Publications, Inc.
1115 Crowley Drive
Carrollton, TX 75011-501010

軍用機、装甲車両、兵士、軍艦などの写真を所持しておられる方はいらっしゃいませんか？どの国のものでも結構です。作戦中に撮影されたものが特に良いのです。Squadron/Signal社の出版する刊行物において、このような写真は内容を一層充実し、興味深くすることができます。当方にお送り頂いた写真は、複写の後お返しいたします。出版物中に写真を使用した場合は、必ず提供者のお名前を明記させて頂きます。お写真は下記にご送付ください。

Squadron/Signal Publications, Inc.
1115 Crowley Drive
Carrollton, TX 75011-501010

Dedication:

To those who fought for Freedom on the Ground, in the Air, and at Sea during the Korean War. Their sacrifice was a shining moment in the history of the world.

Introduction

In September of 1945 the United States was the most powerful nation in the history of the world. With a large, well trained army, a huge navy which plied the world's oceans, an air force which could project airpower over most of the world, and a massive industrial base, America was in a position never before experienced by any other nation in history. When its sole possession of atomic weapons was added, it is easy to see just how powerful the United States was, especially since all the other major powers had been bled dry by World War II. Less scrupulous nations in the past had used such military power to further their own ambition, but the US chose instead to carry out a massive disarmament program and place its faith in the newly created United Nations (UN). Within a year the American military had been cut to the bone. The troops were brought home and released from duty, the ships were mothballed or scrapped, and the vast majority of the aircraft were melted down to get some of their value back in useable metals. There was even some consideration given to turning US nuclear weapons over to UN control.

Yet despite its good intentions the world was not as friendly a place as America wished it to be. Within a few years it began to dawn on the American people and their leaders just how dangerous it was. In Eastern Europe the Soviet Union began to take control of the various countries it had 'liberated' during the war. In 1946 Winston Churchill, the famous British leader, stated that an 'Iron Curtain' had descended over the countries under Russian control. During the summer of 1948 the Russians tried to force the Western allies out of Berlin by blockading the city. Only a massive airlift lasting several months kept the city supplied with food, fuel and medicine and forced the Soviets to eventually back down. Further south, a Soviet backed guerrilla force tried to overthrow the democratically elected government in Greece. Only military aid from both the US and Great Britain allowed the Greek military forces to triumph over the guerrillas. In Asia, China was wracked by a civil war which eventually led to a communist victory. In Indochina and Malaya communist forces were also on the offensive against French and British colonial rule.

In spite of these warning signs, United States political leaders chose to bury their heads in the sand. Little was done to upgrade the military and the defense budget was constantly slashed. Military preparedness dropped and by the end of the decade it was clear that the United States military forces were but a shadow of what they had been only five years earlier. Some political and military leaders tried to change this downward spiral — with little success.

At this critical time a seemingly minor slip by Secretary Of State Dean Acheson had far reaching consequences. During a press conference he outlined America's Far East commitment, including Japan, Okinawa, the Philippines, Australia, and New Zealand. Acheson failed to mention South Korea, a small country which had come to life in the aftermath of World War Two when the Korean peninsula had been temporarily divided at the 38th Parallel to facilitate the disarming of Japanese troops by both American and Russian forces. There were supposed to be free elections to unite the two partitioned sections; however, the Russians continually balked at this idea and refused to abide by earlier agreements. The matter was eventually turned over to the UN, but the Russians were intransigent on the issue. This led to a decision to hold elections in the south which led to the election of Syngman Rhee, a staunch anti-Communist. In response the Soviets declared this election illegal and held their own, electing Kim Il Sung. Each leader vowed to reunite the two Koreas under their leadership, but while the Americans kept Rhee in check, the Russians provided Kim with relatively modern offensive weapons, including tanks, aircraft, and heavy artillery. By contrast the Republic of Korea (ROK) Army was limited by the United States to small arms, light artillery, no armored vehicles, and only trainers and liaison aircraft. By 1948 the Russians had withdrawn their troops from North Korea, followed in mid-1949 by the removal of all American troops from the south. Both sides kept advisors on their respective sides of the border and, as the decade closed, there was a feeling by some that the two countries were on a collision course.

When Acheson left Korea out of his speech as being an area that the United States was committed to protect it sent a message to the North Korean leadership. Recent documents strongly support the theory that the North Koreans would not have attacked had he not left South Korea out of his remarks. Kim Il Sung viewed this omission as a green light to attack, feeling that the United States would not commit its forces to the defense of the South Koreans. Throughout the spring of 1950 the North Korean People's Army (NKPA) began to prepare for the reunification of the two Koreas by force. On 25 June 1950 the North Koreans launched a massive ground assault spearheaded by 150 T-34/85 medium tanks, heavy artillery support, and aircraft. Within days South Korean troops were in headlong retreat. It was soon realized that only an intervention by US forces could repel the communist attack. The only forces which could immediately be brought to bear were the men and aircraft of the Far East Air Force. Consequently, not quite five years after the bloodiest war in history, Americans were again heading into battle. What follows is a story of unpreparedness, mistakes, innovation, and heroism. It is the story of what brave men did to protect a small nation from the threat of naked aggression. In the end it saw the United States act in concert with other countries of the United Nations to throw back the communist attack. The men and women who carried this out were, for the most part, ordinary individuals who just did their job. Yet in doing so they wrote a new chapter in the history of the world which must never be forgotten. For they flew and fought not for personal gain, but to protect freedom under the banner of the United Nations — and in doing so, provided mankind with one of its finest hours.

The one aircraft which perhaps epitomized the Korean War — apart from the F-86 Sabre — was the Douglas B-26 Invader. The B-26 carried out both the first and last official offensive missions against the North Koreans and saw continuous service throughout the conflict. The Invader served as both a day and night bomber and in the reconnaissance role. Designed during World War Two, the B-26 saw limited service toward the end of the war, then went on to provide superb support in Korea. The B-26 ended its career in Vietnam, the only American combat aircraft to see action in all three wars. This Invader unleashes a string of 500 lb (226.8 KG) bombs across Chinese positions in late 1951. With a large payload capacity and fourteen forward firing .50 caliber (12.7MM) machine guns in the nose and wings, the B-26B was a formidable ground support aircraft and wreaked havoc against communist targets throughout the war. (USAF/NA)

1950

Sunday, 25 June 1950, dawned cold and drizzly over the Korean Peninsula. The weather provided cover when the North Korean People's Army (NKPA) unleashed a massive ground offensive against the Republic of Korean (ROK) troops stationed along the 38th Parallel. Spearheaded by Russian made T34/85 medium tanks, one of the finest tank designs at the time, North Korean troops made significant progress against the lightly armed ROK soldiers. Overhead, Russian-built Yak-7 fighters and Ilyushin Il-10 Stormovik attack aircraft of the North Korean Air Force (NKAF) spread out over the peninsula in search of targets of opportunity. At Kimpo airfield the NKAF aircraft caught a Douglas C54 Skymaster of the 374th Troop Carrier Wing on the ground and destroyed it in a series of strafing attacks. The C-54 had been sent to South Korea on the orders of President Truman to help evacuate Americans in South Korea. When word of the attack reached General Douglas MacArthur at his Tokyo headquarters, MacArthur ordered the Far East Air Force (FEAF) to provide fighter cover for future evacuation flights. The FEAF assigned the job to the 8th Fighter-Bomber Wing (FBW) equipped with Lockheed F-80C Shooting Stars and the 4th, 68th, and 339th Fighter (All Weather) Squadrons (F(AW)S) flying North American F-82G Twin Mustangs.

On the morning of 26 June the fighter squadrons began flying cover for the evacuation. In addition to covering the airfields, the F-82s were also ordered to fly cover for the Norwegian merchant ship REINHOLT, then being used as an evacuation vessel. The fighters were also allowed to move inland to cover truck convoys coming from Seoul, the South Korean capital, to Inchon, the port being used by the Norwegian ship. During one of these flights a Yak made a pass at two F-82s, but the US pilots, unsure about the situation, took evasive action and held their fire; the North Korean aircraft flew away. The next day, 27 June, things heated up. While on patrol over Kimpo, F-82s intercepted a flight of Yak fighters intent on strafing transports on the ground and, in a short melee, destroyed two of the North Korean fighters. Credit for the first kill went to Lt William 'Skeeter' Hudson and his radar operator (RO), Lt Carl Fraser although there is some evidence that the first kill was achieved by Lt Charles Moran and his RO Fred Larkins. Moran was killed in action a short time later and in 1953 the Fifth Air Force officially credited Hudson with the first kill of the war. Another Yak was also shot down a few minutes later by Major James Little with two other pilots getting credits for probables.

Undeterred by their first skirmish with American pilots, the North Koreans made another attempt to disrupt the aerial evacuation. Early that afternoon, the NKAF sent a flight of eight Il-10s to attack the transports at Kimpo. Orbiting high overhead were four F-80Cs of the 35th Fighter-Bomber Squadron (FBS). The US jet fighters quickly dropped down and engaged the North Korean aircraft. Within a few minutes four of the Il-10s went down in flames — one each being credited to Captain

Raymond Schillereff and Lt Robert Dewald and two going to Lt Robert Wayne. These four kills were the first aerial victories for American jet fighters and demonstrated the superiority of jets over piston engine aircraft.

While these victories raised morale, the ground war quickly deteriorated for the ROK troops. Lacking tanks and equipped with obsolete anti-tank weapons, the South Korean Army was unable to stop the tank led NKPA assault and began to quickly give ground. Plans were made to provide additional air support in the hopes of stopping the invaders and President Truman authorized the FEAF to commence combat operations on 28 June. In anticipation of this approval, General MacArthur had ordered Boeing B-29 Superfortresses from the 19th Bomb Group (BG) to hit targets near Seoul; these missions were flown on 27 June, the same day that the Yaks and Il-10s had been downed. The day before a WB-29 from the 512th Reconnaissance Squadron (Weather) had flown over North Korean positions to try and get a clear idea of the situation. On 28 June the North Koreans were hit by B-29s, Douglas B-26 Invaders from the 3rd BG, and F-80s. Their targets were enemy troop and vehicle columns heading for Seoul. These early missions highlighted the urgency of the situation. While the B-26s were well suited for tactical support, the B-29s were strategic bombers — their use in a tactical role was essentially a wasted effort in terms of concrete results. The F-80s were not really ground support aircraft, but interceptors; their limited range proved to be a handicap. Flying out of Japan with any type of ordnance restricted the F-80s to only a few minutes over the target. In many instances the jets flew only with their machine-guns to give them more time over target. Nevertheless, the deteriorating ground situation called for desperate measures and the attacks gave notice to the North Koreans that they were not going to roll south unopposed.

Despite FEAF intervention, the North Koreans continued their efforts to disrupt the air evacuation. On 28 June the NKAF hit Suwon, destroying an F-82 and B-26 which had made emergency landings. Later in the day the NKAF returned, destroying one C-54 on the ground and damaging another trying to land. On 29 June the NKAF tried to repeat its success, but ran afoul of patrolling F-80s, which accounted for shooting down an Il-10 and an La-7. Later that afternoon additional NKAF aircraft came in when there was no American fighter cover and destroyed another C-54 during a bombing attack. The long flight time from Japan, coupled with the F-80s limited time over their patrol area, made it possible for the North Korean fighters and bombers to slip in and cause such damage. Additionally, the lack of time over target and inability to carry much ordnance made the F-80s unsuited for these missions as long as they were based in Japan. It would have been ideal if some of them could be based in South Korea, but none of the airfields were capable of sustaining them due to short runways and primitive maintenance facilities.

Consequently, the decision was made to convert a number of the F-80 squadrons back to propeller driven North American F-51 Mustangs and

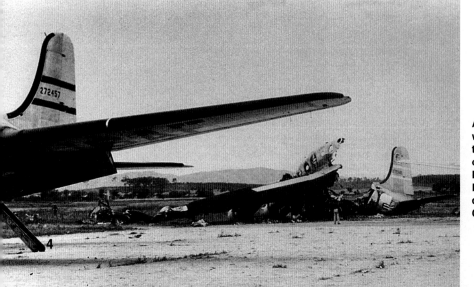

A large number of Americans were in South Korea when the North Koreans launched their attack during the early hours of 25 June 1950. The Americans were ordered evacuated and many were flown out by Douglas C-54 Skymaster transports. Some North Korean fighters slipped past American fighters and destroyed a number of C-54s in strafing attacks. This C-54D was knocked out at Suwon. (USAF/NA)

base them in Korea. President Rhee had also requested ten F-51s be supplied to the ROK Air Force (ROKAF) and these fighters started to arrive in Korea in early July. To help train the ROK pilots, a number of US pilots under the command of Major Dean Hess were assigned to the ROK detachment, eventually designated 'Bout One'. Conditions had so deteriorated on the ground that these F-51s were reclaimed by the US and flew with American pilots while still in their ROK markings. Based at Taegu (K-2), these Mustangs were (for a time) the only tactical aircraft based in Korea due to the possibility of the NKPA overrunning other airfields during the dark days of July. The ROK pilots flew their first official mission in August after on-the-job training with Hess' detachment.

While the ground war continued to go from bad to worse for the South Koreans the decision was reached to commit American ground troops to the conflict. It was realized that the use of US air power in the initial stages was not sufficient to stop the North Korean invasion. The first contingent of troops, Task Force Smith from the 24th Infantry Division, dug in on a series of ridges north of Osan on 4 July, with only a few howitzers and light weapons for support. The next day T34/85s and two regiments of NKPA troops overwhelmed them. There was no air support for the small unit, which would have been of immense help in prolonging their defense of the ridgeline by destroying a large number of T-34s which were neatly lined up in file on the road below their position. This defeat was the first in series suffered by American ground forces which were committed piecemeal, often without adequate support.

Since there were few F-51s left in the Far East, it was decided to collect a large number of Mustangs flying with US Air National Guard (ANG) units and ship these to Japan to help re-equip the FEAF F-80 units. F-51s, collected from across the country, were ferried to Alameda, California. Eventually 145 fighters and 70 pilots were loaded aboard the USS BOXER (CV-21). The BOXER left port on 15 July and eight days later the F-51s were unloading in Tokyo. The maintenance crews in Japan were given two weeks to get all 145 aircraft combat ready. In the meantime a provisional squadron under the project designation 'Dallas' was formed to operate 30 F-51s out of Taegu. Before they could become operational, the 51st Provisional Fighter Squadron was formed at Taegu by the 5th Air Force with orders to absorb both the Bout One and the Dallas units. Additional F-51s were used to equip the 40th FS from the 35th FG, which flew to Pohang (K-3) in mid-July. Both the 40th and the 51st Fighter Squadrons provided outstanding support during the bitter fighting of July. This fighting saw US and ROK forces steadily pushed south toward what was to become known as the Pusan Perimeter.

Additional B-26 and B-29 units were sent to the theater to assist the hard-pressed bomber units, which had been flying near round-the-clock missions in support of the retreating ground forces. In early July the 22nd and 92nd Bomb Groups — both flying B-29s — were ordered to move to Okinawa. By mid-July the two bomb groups were flying strategic missions over North Korea and support missions for American and ROK troops in the south. By the beginning of August, two additional B-29 units, the 98th and 307th Bomb Groups, were deployed to Korea — within five days they too were flying combat missions. With the 3rd Bomb Group heavily committed to both day and night bombing missions, it was decided to activate the 452nd BG, a California Air National Guard unit. Unfortunately the unit needed both reinforcement and additional training; it was not until late October that the unit began flying combat in Korea. One of its four squadrons was assigned to the 3rd BG to bring that unit up to strength.

Additional help was also on the way to blunt the North Korean offensive. No 77 Squadron of the Royal Australian Air Force (RAAF), equipped with F-51s was stationed in Japan on occupation duty. When hostilities broke out their help was requested, but they could not be released for combat until Great Britain took an official stand. This was quickly given and on 2 July No 77 Squadron flew their first combat missions. The squadron was later assigned to the 35th FG and staged out of Taegu until moving to Pohang (K-3) in early October. More help was forthcoming from another quarter. On 3 July aircraft from Task Force (TF) 77 composed of the USS VALLEY FORGE (CV-45) and HMS TRIUMPH hit airfields and lines of communications in North Korea near its capital, Pyongyang, and Onjong-ni. Two Yak-9s were downed by F9F-3s and ten more aircraft were destroyed on the ground near Pyongyang. Good results were also achieved against the ground targets. Supplementing the naval effort was the assignment of Patrol Squadron 47 (VP-47) to patrol duty off the Korean coast with their PBM-5 Mariners. VP-47 was later reinforced by the P2V-2 Neptunes of VP-6. Both naval patrol squadrons began to carry out bombing and reconnaissance missions until relieved when additional units arrived in the theater. VP-47 and VP-6 then resumed normal patrol flights in support of fleet operations.

Despite the air power buildup, the North Koreans continued to roll on, pushing the beleaguered defenders further south. By this time the United Nations had sanctioned the use of military force to throw back the invaders and General MacArthur was appointed commander of all forces in the theater. Throughout July MacArthur rushed American units to Korea as fast as possible in an attempt to stem the tide. Under the command of General Walton Walker, the Eighth Army slowly took shape. Lacking heavy armor to stop the T-34s, air power played a vital role in slowing down the North Koreans. Napalm proved an ideal weapon to destroy the Russian-made tanks, which became prime targets for the Air Force and Navy aircraft. Reinforcements slowly began to arrive from the US and included the 1st Marine Provisional Brigade with its own air support — Marine Air Group 33 (MAG-33). Long proponents of close air-ground support, the Marines proved to be the key to holding the final UN position along the Naktong River, the Pusan Perimeter.

In the meantime, additional F-80 units were converting to F-51s. The

Some US and foreign citizens were evacuated from South Korea on the Norwegian freighter REINHOLT. The ship was protected by USAF F-82s until it reached US Navy destroyers waiting offshore. The REINHOLT and her escorts then proceeded to Japan, with additional air cover for the convoy provided by B-26s. (USAF/NA)

arrival of the USS BOXER with its load of Mustangs allowed the 40th FS's sister unit, the 39th FS, to exchange their F-80s and move to Pohang (K-3) in early August. The 18th FBG, based in the Philippines, dispatched the 67th FS to Japan, where they picked up their F-51s and deployed to Taegu. Once in place, the 51st FS was redesignated the 12th FS after the unit which had originally supplied most of the new unit's pilots in the first place. The 12th FS then rejoined the 18th FBG. The last units to convert to the F-51s were the 35th and 36th FSs of the 8th FBG. These two squadrons changed over in early August and flew their initial missions out of Japan. In a little over a month, the 5th Air Force had converted six squadrons under wartime conditions to the F-51, a remarkable transition given the time and problems facing them. All of these squadrons were needed since the fighting continued to heat up around the ever-shrinking United Nations enclave.

The Pusan Perimeter and Inchon

By late August of 1950 the Eighth Army had been pushed back into a small corner of southeastern Korea — an area roughly 50 by 80 miles. A continuous line, thinly manned, was able to hold out against the North Koreans who had expected to quickly overrun the South. In part, the resistance of the US and ROK ground forces had thwarted their expectations of an easy victory, but a large degree of the credit had to go to the air power thrown against them. Without it the North Koreans would have been successful. Nevertheless, while it had blunted the communist drive, air power alone could not achieve victory without ground troops, a factor which was (and sometimes still is) often overlooked by Air Force officers. Ground and air power worked together and were mutually dependent on one another, something which the Marines had worked long and hard to perfect and had used with great success during the battle for the Pusan Perimeter. The Air Force and Army were relearning this concept and developing a working relationship when the war began its third month.

In addition to providing direct support to the troops, the fighter-bombers were also used to interdict the North Korean's lines of supply and communications. These lines were also the targets of the B-26s and B29s that ranged far north of the perimeter in an attempt to isolate the troops attacking the UN enclave from their supply points. It became almost impossible for the communists to move men and material except under the cover of darkness. Additionally, major strategic targets were hit — manufacturing plants, oil storage sites, and airfields — to deprive the North Koreans of the means to wage war. When the fighting finally stabilized around the Pusan Perimeter, the NKPA was a shell of its former self; few T-34 tanks were left and the troops had been decimated by air strikes and ground fire. In some cases South Koreans had been impressed into the communist ranks and many of the remaining soldiers were equipped with weapons captured or abandoned by the retreating American and South Korean troops. The NKPA still held a psychologi-cal advantage, but this waned when the American and South Koreans held their ground and threw back the NKPA assaults along the Naktong.

One of the early problems faced by the F-51s and the F-80s had been the inability to find suitable targets. This was especially hard for the F-80s given their limited time over the battlefield. In early July of 1950 tests were conducted using T-6 trainers fitted with eight channel AN/ARC-3 radio sets to direct fighter-bombers against ground targets. It was felt that T-6s were better suited for this role than light liaison aircraft, several of which had been shot down by North Korean fighters. The T-6s were much faster and better able to evade the NKAF fighters. These tests proved successful and by mid-July, the T-6s were operating over the battlefield with good results. The T-6s were initially given the call sign 'Mosquito'. The name stuck and the T-6 units became known as 'Mosquito' squadrons. These Forward Air Controllers (FACs) became an indispensable part of the air war and were hated by the North Koreans for the death they brought down on them. FAC pilots shot down and captured by the communist troops often faced a horrible death in reprisal. Supplementing the airborne FACs were pilots assigned to ground units as Forward Observers (FOs). FOs helped direct air strikes on targets close to their assigned units. This practice had been finely tuned by the Marines over the years, but had to be relearned by the Army and Air Force despite the concept's proven success in World War Two. The use of the FACs and FOs also helped cut down on accidental air strikes against UN troops — an event which had occurred all too frequently during the early days of the war.

By early September of 1950, the war had reached a stalemate around the Pusan perimeter. Neither side was capable of dislodging the other although the tide had swung in favor of the American and ROK forces. Reinforcements, including Commonwealth troops, were arriving to reinforce the UN forces, but the immediate prospects for a reversal of fortunes was not anticipated any time soon. While the Eighth Army doggedly held their line along the Naktong, plans were underway to bring a speedy end to the war at MacArthur's headquarters in Tokyo. The plan involved a major amphibious attack against the port of Inchon west of Seoul. If successful, this landing would cut off the North Korean troops at the Pusan Perimeter and force them to retreat or be destroyed in place.

The US Navy moved a powerful carrier force into Korean waters to support the Inchon landings. These carriers included the USS VALLEY FORGE, just returned from a replenishment call at Okinawa, the USS PHILIPPINE SEA (CV-47), the USS BADOENG STRAITS (CVE-116), the USS SICILY (CVE-118), and the British carrier HMS TRIUMPH. The two CVEs had Marine fighter squadrons on board for close support of the embarked troops, while the British ship served in the blockade and support role. The two fleet carriers provided the main nucleus of the strike force for the fleet. In anticipation of the invasion, the Marine Brigade was pulled out of the perimeter to form up with the 1st Marine Division, the spearhead of the ground force. Its removal from the line was a gamble — the North Koreans still held their psychological advantage around the enclave. Thanks to the air support rendered by the fighter-bombers and the interdiction of the NKPA's long supply lines by the B-26s and B-29s, the North Korean troops were really at the end of their rope and were hanging on

On 27 June 1950 patrolling North American F-82 Twin Mustangs were over Kimpo when five North Korean Yak-9Ps tried to disrupt the aerial evacuation. In the melee which followed, the Americans shot down three of the Yakovlev fighters. Lt William Hudson (left) received official credit for the first kill along with his R/O (Radar Officer), Lt Carl Fraser (right). Between them are the crewmen credited for the second kill, Lt Charles Moran (left center) and his R/O, Lt Fred Larkins. (USAF/NA)

C-54 transports airlifted Detachment X from the 507th Anti-Aircraft Battalion to bolster airfield defense at Suwon. These troops have set up a M55 Quad .50 caliber machine gun mount to protect the airstrip from strafing fighters. The B-26B and Lt Moran's F-82 are parked on the hardstand after each aircraft made emergency landings at Suwon. Behind them is the wreck of the C-54 shown in the photograph on page 4. (USA/NA)

by sheer guts alone. The timing was just right for a counterattack.

One fear facing UN forces was the possible intervention of either Russian or Chinese forces, particularly air units into the fighting. On 4 September, radar spotted a flight of unidentified aircraft approaching the fleet in the Yellow Sea from the direction of the Russian naval base at Port Arthur. Corsairs from the VALLEY FORGE, vectored toward the group, split up, one group turning back while the other group continued on. When spotted by the Corsairs, the intruder, wearing Russian markings, opened fire. The Corsairs returned fire and shot it down. One body was recovered and later turned over to the Russians who claimed that it was a training mission gone awry.

Against this tense backdrop the fleet approached Inchon in mid-September. On 15 September elements of the 1st Marine Division landed and secured a beachhead. The Marines quickly pushed inland and by 17 September had recaptured Kimpo Airfield (K-14). By 20 September elements of VMF-212, equipped with Corsairs, and VMF(N)-542, flying F7F-3N Tigercats, were conducting missions in support of the ground troops. With Kimpo secured, additional Marine Corsairs came in and USAF C-54s and C-119 'Flying Boxcars' began to bring in supplies and take out wounded.

At the Pusan Perimeter the Eighth Army began its breakout on 16 September — the day after the Inchon landings. In some cases the units of the Eighth Army had to repel NKPA attacks before beginning their own offensive. After some intense fighting, the NKPA began to break, particularly when word of the Inchon landing was received. In some cases there was wholesale flight to escape the attacking UN forces. The fighter-bombers had a field day when the communist troops came out in the open and they decimated them. By 26 September, units of both forces had linked up. Two days later Seoul was declared officially secured. The front lines gradually began to stabilize and plans were made to continue the drive north and reunify the country under President Rhee.

North To The Yalu

With the decision to drive toward the Yalu River (the Chinese/North Korean border) additional F-51s and F-80s were transferred from Japan to South Korea in order to lessen the flight time to their targets. The 49th FBG, flying from Taegu, became the first F-80 unit to operate out of Korea in late September. The 49th FBG was followed by the 51st FG at Kimpo in late October. The 51st FG was joined a few days later by F-51s from the 35th and 36th FSs. The fighter-bombers began a massive support effort for the UN ground forces pushing north across the 38th Parallel toward the North Korean capital of Pyongyang and the Yalu River. The fighter-bombers also ranged far ahead of the ground forces in search of retreating enemy columns and flew escort for B-29 missions against distant targets in the north.

It appeared that things were well in hand and, although everyone began to think in terms of being home by Christmas, there were some ominous signs that not all was right. On several occasions unidentified jets were observed high overhead while the fighter-bombers searched for targets down low. At airfields across the Yalu in Manchuria large numbers of aircraft were seen at the airfield complex around Antung. Then, on 1 November, four F-51s of the 67th FBS were jumped by six MiG-15s north of Sinanju while working with a Mosquito FAC. Turning into the faster jets the F-51s were credited with three probables before the MiGs flew back across the Yalu. Over the next week aerial combat intensified and six Yak fighters were knocked down. Five MiGs were also damaged and Major Kendall Carlson of the 12th FBS may have shot down one on 7 November. Official credit for the first MiG-15 kill was given to Lt Russell Brown. Brown was flying top cover in an F-80 during a strike against Sinanju when he engaged and knocked down a MiG on 8 November. Russian after action reports indicate that this MiG was only damaged and managed to return to base; however, the appearance of the MiG-15 ushered in a new phase of the air war. Neither the F-51s nor F-80s were capable of taking on the Russian jets on equal terms. A call went out for help.

The only American aircraft comparable to the MiG-15 was the North

Four strafing Yaks destroyed Lt Charles Moran's F-82G on the ground at Suwon on 28 June. The Twin Mustang was the first fighter lost by the USAF in the war and demonstrated to the Americans the need to do something about the North Korean Air Force. (USAF/NA)

Three Boeing B-29s carried out a bombing strike against targets around Seoul on 27 June — 24 hours before President Truman gave official permission to do so. One of the bombers was ATOMIC TOM, based on the cat character from Hanna-Barbera's cartoon 'Tom and Jerry.' The bombers were from the 93rd Bombardment Squadron (BS), 19th Bombardment Group (BG). (Dunderdale)

"DOUBLE WHAMMY" was another of the B-29s involved in the strike in the Seoul area. This Superfortress' name was based on the character from Al Capp's cartoon strip 'Evil Eye Fleagle.' This B-29 was lost on 22 January 1952. The 19th BG was based at Kadena Air Base, Okinawa. (USAF/NA)

American F-86A Sabre. In response to the MiG threat the 4th Fighter Interceptor Wing (FIW) was deployed to Korea and the unit began to move cross-country from its bases along the East Coast to San Diego, California. Along the way the 4th FIG gathered the best airframes it could find from other F-86 units and exchanged aircraft. In San Diego the fighters were loaded aboard the USS CAPE ESPERANCE (CVE-88) which arrived in Japan in early December. Salt water had caused much damage to the exposed aircraft and it took some two weeks to get the aircraft combat ready. On 13 December a small detachment of seven F-86As flew into Kimpo, the only base suitable for F-86 operations and two days later flew a combat orientation flight. No MiGs were sighted, but on 17 December a flight of four Sabres led by Lt Col Bruce Hinton encountered four MiG-15s. Hinton shot one down in a swirling dogfight. On 22 December a large-scale engagement took place between the Sabres and the MiGs. Outnumbered two-to-one, the F-86 pilots shot down six MiGs without loss. By the end of the month the 4th FIW had shot down eight MiGs and had two probables for the loss of one F-86.

To help support the Sabres — and give some much needed relief to the F-51s and F-80s — a request was put in for the new Republic F-84 Thunderjet. Although not equal to the MiG-15 in terms of air-to-air combat, the F-84 was still faster than the F-80, had a longer range, could

carry more ordnance, and was capable of absorbing tremendous battle damage. On 11 November 1950, the 27th Fighter Escort Wing (FEW) based at Bergstrom AFB, Texas and equipped with F-84Es, was ordered to Korea. The unit's aircraft were loaded onto the USS BATAAN (CVL-29) and departed for Japan, arriving there at the end of the month.

These reinforcements were much needed; starting in late October the UN ground forces had begun to encounter Chinese 'volunteers' in sizeable numbers. Despite these encounters intelligence did not really consider these troops a serious threat. General MacArthur ordered the UN advance to continue despite some setbacks and the UN forces gradually pushed closer to the Chinese border. Some ROK and American units actually reached the Yalu. On 24 November the final push north was ordered and for two days all went well. Then, on 26 November the Chinese unleashed a massive attack against the Eighth Army. The Eighth Army was unprepared for such an attack. Aerial reconnaissance had not detected the Chinese buildup and the troops were caught totally unaware. The ROK units disintegrated under the onslaught, which exposed the Eighth Army's flank and forced it to retreat in disarray.

The 27th FEW was originally intended to operate out of Kimpo, but the sudden Chinese intervention in late November placed the field in danger. Part of the 27th FEW was then based at Taegu under the com-

The first *official* B-29 attack occurred on 28 June, when a flight of Superfortresses hit targets around Seoul. The first aircraft to drop bombs on that date was CREAM OF THE CROP, a B-29 assigned to the 30th BS, 19th BG. (Dunderdale)

The 19th BG's Commanding Officer did not appreciate the CREAM OF THE CROP's well-endowed artwork and ordered select portions of her anatomy covered up. The ground crew covered just enough of the artwork to make the CO happy and wrote CENSORED on the black patch to show their displeasure. (Dunderdale)

Men and equipment are unloaded from a C-54D (42-72694) of the 374th Troop Carrier Wing under the watchful eyes of a 40mm gun crew. South Korean troops were in full retreat within a week of the war's start. In order to bolster their spirits, two infantry companies from the 24th Infantry Division – designated 'Task Force Smith' – were flown with some artillery and vehicles from Japan to Korea in C-54 transports. Lacking air cover or armor support, 'Task Force Smith' was routed north of Osan on 5 July, losing some 33 percent of its men and most of its equipment. (USAF/NA)

mand of Col Donald Blakeslee. The Wing flew its first mission — against targets near Chinnampo, southwest of Pyongyang — on 7 December with good results.

Air support proved vital in helping to extract trapped units, but inclement weather severely restricted what could be provided; in many cases the ground units had to fend for themselves despite Herculean efforts on the part of the aircrews.

On the eastern side of the peninsula the Marines ran into similar difficulties. After their successful landing at Inchon and capture of Seoul, the Marines had redeployed to the eastern side for an amphibious assault against the port of Wonsan. Providing offshore support were the fleet carriers USS BOXER, USS LEYTE, USS PHILIPPINE SEA, and USS VALLEY FORGE. The HMS THESEUS replaced the HMS TRIUMPH during the first week of October and joined the US carriers in attacks against North Korean targets. Corsairs from VMF-214 and 323 flew into Wonsan to provide close support from airfields secured by ROK troops while the Marines waited offshore for the mines to be cleared. They were finally able to land on 24 October and began to move north toward the Chosin Reservoir. Additional air units, including VMF(N)-513 and VMO-6 flew into Wonsan Airfield, which, by the end of the month, had been equipped with landing lights for night operations. While the Marines moved farther north, the fighter squadrons moved to Yonpo airfield to be closer to the advancing ground forces. Chinese troops began to be encountered when the Marines pushed toward the Yalu River in late October and early November. To stem the flow of enemy troops and reinforcements, it was decided to destroy the Yalu River bridges linking northern Korea and Manchuria.

Beginning on 8 November, a massive series of air strikes was launched using both tactical aircraft and B-29s. The air strikes against the bridges, while successful, did little to hinder the Chinese who had already moved massive mounts of troops and supplies into northern Korea undetected. (Within a week the Yalu had frozen over and the Chinese were able to move additional material across river without difficulty.)

On 9 November Lt Commander W.T. Amen, the CO of VF-111 based on the PHILIPPINE SEA, shot down a MiG-15 in his F9F-2 Panther. Russian records claim this was the first MiG lost during the war, which – if true – would give the credit for the first MiG kill to Amen rather than Lt Russell Brown in his F-80.

Air support became indispensable in slowing down the North Korean advance into the south. Initially, the only tactical aircraft based in South Korea were ten North American F-51 Mustangs flying out of Taegu under the command of Major Dean Hess. Hess and his American pilots were supposed to be training South Korean pilots to fly the F-51, yet ended up flying missions in support of the 24th Infantry Division during its retreat. Korean markings were superimposed over the US insignia on these Mustangs. (USAF/NA)

Initially, all F-51 flying and maintenance was done by USAF personnel due to the critical need for the aircraft to support both US and Republic of Korea (ROK) troops. The South Koreans eventually formed the 1st Fighter Wing, which was equipped with Mustangs and flew ground support missions for UN troops. When the war ended, South Korea was the only nation in the theater still flying Mustangs in frontline service. (USAF/NA)

Lockheed F-80 Shooting Stars based in Japan provided early close air support, although their time over target was limited due to the aircraft's range. This F-80C (47-526) from the 49th Fighter-Bomber Group (FBG) lifts off from Itazuke, Japan, since there were no airfields in South Korea capable of handling jet aircraft. The fighter is carrying only a few rockets and has the new 'Misawa' tip tanks (named for the manufacturing location), which helped extend range and gave the F-80s more time over the battlefield. (USAF/NA)

Sufficient numbers of F-51s were acquired from stateside units to form several squadrons based in Korea, including this aircraft at Taegu. Operating close to the front, the Mustangs were able to react quickly when ground units called for air support. Parked at the far end of the field are Mustangs assigned to No. 77 Squadron, Royal Australian Air Force (RAAF), which were based in Japan on occupation duties when the Korean War began. (USAF/NA)

On the ground, the Marines had deliberately slowed their advance toward the Chosin Reservoir despite urges from MacArthur's headquarters to move more quickly. The Marines suspected a trap along the narrow mountain road which was their sole axis of advance — events were to prove them right. On 28 November the Chinese launched a massive attack consisting of seven divisions against the 1st Marine Division. Although the Marines were able to hold out they were surrounded and faced possible annihilation. In true Marine tradition they did not falter, but instead began a methodical retreat, fighting as they went, bringing out their wounded and in many cases even their dead. Overhead, both Navy and Marine aircraft provided massive cover, attacking the Chinese wherever they were spotted. These fliers inflicted horrendous casualties on the Chinese troops and it is highly unlikely that the Marines would have made it to the coast without this outstanding effort. Even at night the aircraft of VMF(N)-513 and 542 were overhead, providing both physical and moral support to the trapped Marines. Air Force, Navy, and Marine cargo aircraft brought in food and ammunition to the surrounded troops and took out the wounded using a series of crude runways which the Marines had the foresight to build during their initial advance. Old TBM-3 Avengers were used to fly out casualties from the small airstrip at Koto-ri. On 4 December Lt(JG) Thomas Hudner won the Congressional Medal of Honor for crash landing his Corsair next to his wingman, Ensign Jessie Brown — the US Navy's first black aviator. Brown had been shot down by ground fire. Hudner's heroic efforts did not save Brown who was trapped in the cockpit of his Corsair and eventually Hudner was forced to leave when nightfall approached. Hudner was picked up by a VMO-6 rescue helicopter which had tried to assist in the rescue. The next day a flight of Corsairs returned to the scene and used napalm to incinerate Brown's body and his Corsair.

With the help of air support the Marines gradually began to pull back from their positions at Chosin. Moving systematically down the narrow mountain road the leathernecks withdrew to the south, gathering up units strung out along the route. By 6 December, the Marine columns had reached Hagaru; two days later they reached Koto-ri, the last stop before reaching safety. Unfortunately, the Chinese had destroyed a major bridge south of the town and this threatened to stop the retreat cold. The US Air Force, using C-119s, dropped replacement bridge spans by parachute. The spans were moved into place, which allowed the Marines to break

An F-51 taxis out for a mission during August of 1950, armed with a 500 lb bomb and three 5 inch rockets under each wing. Mustangs were able to carry far more ordnance than the F-80s and proved ideal for ground support. F-51s could carry bombs, rockets, and napalm, and loiter over the battlefield for hours in search of targets. Their one drawback was the vulnerability of their inline engine's cooling system to ground fire. (USAF/NA)

The Soviet T-34/85 medium tank was the NKPA's most deadly weapon. This tank, a veteran of World War II, was greatly feared by both US and South Korean troops, who initially had no weapons with which to destroy it. Napalm was the most effective weapon against T-34s — a direct hit was not needed due to the coverage napalm gave when it hit the ground. This T-34 was the victim of a napalm attack near Suwon. (USAF/NA)

North American T-6 Texan trainers were used in the Forward Air Controller (FAC) role to locate and mark targets for the fighter-bombers. The T-6s were extremely effective in this role and provided a vital link between the ground and air units. The Texan in the background was among a few T-6s camouflaged to reduce their visibility to North Korean fighters, which occasionally got past covering USAF fighters. (USAF/NA)

out and reach the safety of the port city of Hungnam where they were evacuated. With the help of air support the Marines were able to inflict nearly 40,000 casualties on the Chinese which blunted their attack and allowed other UN forces to be safely extracted. Without this support it would have been impossible for the Marine and Army troops to have been rescued; the Chinese might well have been able to drive UN forces off the peninsula.

When 1950 came to a close the United States and its allies faced a completely new war both in the air and on the ground. The intervention of Chinese ground troops and the introduction of the MiG-15 totally changed the complexity of the war. The future of the war perhaps looked even gloomier than it had looked during the early summer. Air power had been instrumental in saving the situation numerous times during the hectic retreat and holding action around Pusan. When the UN forces took the offensive, it was equally instrumental in the decimation of the NKPA in the drive north. In turn air power helped provide some breathing space to these same forces when the Chinese counterattacked. It now faced an even greater challenge: the very existence of the ground forces would depend on the ability of the Air Force, Navy, Marine, and allied airmen to help blunt the communist drive that was once again pushing relentlessly south.

F-80s began to stage out of Taegu during the day and returned to Japan at night to provide better coverage and more time over the front lines. Two F-80Cs from the 35th Fighter Interceptor Wing (FIW) take off with a load of rockets on a tank-hunting mission in August of 1950. Although rockets could destroy a T-34 if one hit the tank's rear deck, they were not particularly accurate — napalm was still the best weapon against the Soviet-built vehicle. (USAF/NA)

One the war's best close air support aircraft was the Douglas B-26 Invader, which could carry a large array of ordnance over long distances. With six or eight .50 caliber (12.7MM) machine guns in the nose and six more weapons in the wings, the Invader was the ultimate strafer. A large internal bomb load, backed up by wing racks – which could carry rockets, bombs, and napalm – made the B-26 one of the most deadly aircraft of the war. B-26s of the 3rd BG carried out the first official raid north of the 38th Parallel on 28 June. (USAF/NA)

While the fighter-bombers carried the war to the enemy down low, B-29s carried out attacks against strategic targets both north and south of the 38th Parallel – hitting bridges, oil storage facilities, troop concentrations, and rail lines. These Superfortresses from the 92nd BG head for a target near Pyongyang in early August of 1950. Each of the five B-29 groups operating over Korea had distinctive tail codes to provide easy identification to fellow airmen. (USAF/NA)

US and British aircraft carriers, assigned to Task Force 77 off the Korean coast, provided additional air support to the hard-pressed UN ground forces. A Douglas AD-4Q Skyraider from VF-55 and a Vought F4U-4B Corsair assigned to VF-54 landed at Taegu to refuel and rearm before returning to the USS VALLEY FORGE (CV-45). Using South Korean airfields enabled Navy pilots to get in a double strike against the North Koreans and allowed greater flexibility in mission planning and aircraft utilization. (USN/NA)

US Aircraft Carriers Assigned to Task Force 77 During the Korean War

USS ESSEX (CV-9)
USS YORKTOWN (CV-10)
USS BOXER (CV-21)
USS BON HOMME RICHARD (CV-31)
USS LEYTE (CV-32)
USS KEARSARGE (CVA-33)
USS ORISKANY (CVA-34)
USS ANTIETAM (CV-36)
USS PRINCETON (CV-37)
USS LAKE CHAMPLAIN (CV-39)
USS VALLEY FORGE (CV-45)
USS PHILIPPINE SEA (CV-47)
USS BATAAN (CVL-29)
USS SICILY (CVE-118)
USS POINT CRUZ (CVE-119)
USS RENDOVA (CVE-114)
USS BAIROKO (CVE-115)

While US and Allied forces tried to stem the tide of the North Korean assault, reinforcements were on the way. Marine F4U Corsairs from VMF-214 are hoisted aboard the escort carrier USS SICILY (CVE-118) shortly after the war began. SICILY was commanded by Captain Jimmy Thach, the famous World War II ace who developed the 'Thach Weave' to help Navy pilots fight the Japanese Zero fighter. (USN/NA)

Marine Air Group 33 (MAG-33) operated in support of the 1st Provisional Marine Brigade during the defense of the Pusan Perimeter. An F4U Corsair assigned to MAG-33 comes in from the left for a bomb run against North Korean troops and tanks. The large columns of black smoke are from previous napalm attacks. (USMC/NA)

The turning point of the war came in September of 1950, when General Douglas MacArthur launched a surprise amphibious invasion at Inchon, west of Seoul. Pushing inland, the Marines captured Kimpo airfield on 17 September. The first aircraft to land at Kimpo after its capture was this Corsair from VMF–214 flown by Lt John Hanes, which had been damaged by ground fire. Forty mission markers are painted just forward of the windshield. (USMC/NA)

The twisted, burnt out remains of this North Korean Il-10 were discovered along the side of Kimpo's runway, the victim of a strafing attack a few hours before the US landing at Inchon. The Ilyushin Il-10 was the final version of the famous Il-2 Stormovik, one of finest ground attack aircraft of World War II. (USMC/NA)

The Inchon assault resulted in the complete rout of the North Korean forces and UN troops rapidly pursued them north across the 38th Parallel. During the advance to the north, additional reinforcements were on the way to upgrade the UN air forces. Republic F-84E Thunderjets began to replace F-51s in fighter-bomber units in late November. These F-84s are from the 27th Fighter Escort Wing (FEW) under the command of World War II ace Col Don Blakeslee. The nose, tail, and tip tank markings were red. (USAF/NA)

RAAF Mustangs prepare for takeoff on a ground support mission shortly after the Chinese entered the Korean War in late November of 1950. The Chinese launched a surprise attack against UN forces advancing towards the Yalu River. The sudden appearance of large numbers of Chinese troops caught MacArthur by surprise and forced a hasty retreat by UN ground forces. Air power played a key role in saving the UN ground forces from annihilation by numerically superior Chinese forces. (USAF/NA)

Nowhere was air power more important than the Chosin Reservoir, where the 1st Marine Division was surrounded by seven Chinese divisions. This F4U-5N from VMF-513 flew 80 day and night missions in support of the Marines during their breakout from the huge Chinese trap. The aircraft is fitted with radar in the starboard fuselage pod and is armed with eight 5 inch rockets under the wings. (USMC/NA)

Cold Marines watch a Corsair drop a load of napalm on Chinese positions overlooking the main road south out of the Chosin Reservoir area. The 1st Marine Division's main support came from Navy carrier aircraft and Marine aircraft based at Yonpo airfield near Hungnam. Upon breaking out from the Chosin Reservoir, the Marines advanced towards the port of Hungnam, where they were evacuated. (USMC/NA)

US Air Force transports flew in tons of ammunition and supplies for the Marines and evacuated casualties to hospitals in Japan. A variety of transports – including Curtiss C-46 Commandos, Douglas C-54 Skymasters, and Fairchild C-119 Flying Boxcars – pack Yonpo during the retreat and evacuation. (USMC/NA)

An F4U-4B from VMF-212 taxies past other Corsairs before a mission over the withdrawing Marine column. The Marines were forced to advance along a single mountain road, which provided the Chinese with several ideal ambush positions. Constant patrols were kept over the column to spot and attack any Chinese forces which tried to interfere with the Marine withdrawal. (USMC/NA)

This Lockheed P2V-3 Neptune flew over Marine positions at night, dropping flares to provide illumination for attacking aircraft and troops on the ground. Neptunes were used in patrol, attack, and observation roles during the war. Eventually, seven Neptune squadrons would see service in Korea. (USMC/NA)

Two Grumman TBM-3E Avengers – this one is running its engine – used the advance airstrip at Koto-Ri to evacuate casualties during the breakout from the Chosin Reservoir. In a six-day period, Captain Alfred McCaleb of VMO-6 and Lt Truman Clark of VMF(N)-513 flew out 103 wounded Marines to Yonpo for evacuation to hospitals in Japan. (USMC/NA)

Off shore, the US fleet endured horrendous winter weather, which made flight operations extremely dangerous. These Corsairs and Skyraiders sit on the snow-covered aft deck of the USS PHILIPPINE SEA (CV-47) in late November. Pilots going down in the frigid waters off the Korean coast had a life expectancy measured in minutes. (USN/NA)

Ground crew refuel this Grumman F9F-2B Panther assigned to VMF-311 at Yonpo. The Panther is armed with four air-to-ground rockets under the port wing and four 20MM cannons in the nose. VMF-311 was the first Marine jet squadron and flew missions out of Yonpo from 10 through 14 December. (USMC/NA)

In late November of 1950, South Africa began operations using F-51s of No. 2 Squadron. The unit was assigned to the US 18th Fighter Bomber Wing (FBW) and flew their first mission out of Taegu (K-2), then moved to Pyongyang East just as the Chinese were launching their massive ground attack. No. 2 Squadron was better known as the 'Flying Cheetahs,' after the two cheetah cubs the South Africans brought with them as mascots. (USAF/NA)

The air war took a new turn in November, when Soviet-built MiG-15s were encountered. No UN aircraft in the theater was comparable to this fast, swept wing fighter. To counter the MiG threat, the 4th FIW was rushed from the US to Korea. The Wing was flying the best fighter in the USAF inventory, the North American F-86A Sabre. These Sabres are being prepared for a fighter sweep out of Kimpo over northwest Korea near the Yalu River — known for the next three years as 'MiG Alley.' (USAF/NA)

17

1951

By the start of the New Year the Chinese had launched a major offensive against the Allied Eighth Army which, despite massive air support, fell back quickly in the face of overwhelming odds. By 5 January Seoul had fallen once again and Kimpo airbase was lost. The UN retreat continued south of the Han River with the front finally stabilizing between Pyongtaek and Samchok by the middle of the month. The Chinese advance forced a number of the F-80 squadrons and the F-86s to pull out of Kimpo and relocate to Japan. The extreme range prevented the Sabres from providing cover for the fighter-bombers, which ventured north to the area of northwest Korean air space which became known as 'MiG Alley.' The MiGs became more aggressive and shot down or damaged a number of F-80s and F-84s, but on 21 January the CO of the 523rd FES, Lt Col William Bertram, shot down a MiG, the first of nine to fall to the slower Thunderjets. Two days later the F-84s of the 27th FEW struck the airfield at Sinuiju on the North Korean side of the Yalu across from the main MiG base at Antung. Thirty MiG-15s intercepted the F-84s after they completed their bombing mission. In the swirling dogfight which followed, the F84 pilots claimed four kills, three probables, and four damaged. The USAF claims board eventually gave credit for two kills and five probables. Nevertheless, this was a creditable performance by the F-84s over the MiG-15s. The F-84 pilots were able to take advantage of their superior training and the better maneuverability of the Thunderjets at low altitude where they could turn inside the faster Russian fighters.

Despite the success of the F-84s, the only real answer to the MiG threat was the F-86 — and these were desperately needed over the battlefield in order to regain and maintain air superiority for the UN forces. In early March the problem of range was somewhat eliminated when some F-86s began to stage out of Suwon to increase their loitering time over 'MiG Alley,' while other Sabres operated out of Taegu. The problem of distance still precluded joint operations. Eventually the Taegu based Sabres began flying from Suwon in April of 1951, which made it easier to coordinate missions and provide more effective coverage.

Off the coast, the Navy provided much needed support for the United Nations ground forces during their withdrawal down the Korean peninsula. All through the months of January and February aircraft from Task Force 77 hit Chinese troops and supply points — strikes which helped slow down the communist ground advance. In late February the UN troops mounted OPERATION KILLER which drove the Chinese back and resulted in the recapture of Seoul. By the end of April, KILLER had pushed the enemy back across the 38th Parallel, but the resilient Chinese then launched a counterattack which pushed the UN troops back again. This was followed by yet another UN counterattack which then pushed the Chinese back across the 38th Parallel. The line at which the UN offensive halted would be, for all intents and purposes, the front line for the next two years with only minor changes.

Throughout the ebb and flow nature of the fighting, both naval and air force aircraft played an important part in keeping the enemy from building up sufficient supplies and troop concentrations to overwhelm the UN ground forces. When the Chinese were able to break through the lines and force a retreat, the fighter-bombers were quick to pounce on any worthwhile target which made it difficult for the Chinese to carry out any attack in depth for any length of time. Additionally, air power helped decimate enemy troops when they came out of their hiding places to attack and often were the only reason that friendly ground units were able to survive at all against the overwhelming 'human wave' attacks favored by the communists.

When the front line began to stabilize the air war moved into a series of generalized missions. The first priority was to maintain control of the air, the second was to provide direct support for the ground troops along the front line, the third was to hit enemy targets behind the main-line-of-resistance (MLR), and finally to provide information on enemy forces and targets. Subsidiary missions — casualty evacuation, rescue of downed pilots, and supply missions — fell under these general headings and formed the backdrop for the next two years of the aerial conflict.

One of the most demanding missions for all the units involved was the effort to deny enemy forces the supplies they needed to function: food, fuel, and ammunition. OPERATION STRANGLE was begun in the spring of 1951 and aimed at key enemy supply lines. Utilizing Air Force, Navy, and Marine air aircraft, STRANGLE was designed to cut the flow of enemy supplies between the 39th Parallel and the MLR. Initially quite successful, the operation lost effectiveness when the communists mustered large numbers of troops and workers to rebuild rail lines, roads, and bridges. North of the targeted area other fighter-bombers, B-26s, and B-29s hit key transportation junctions, supply points, airfields, and other strategic targets in order to keep the pressure on the communists. One such target was the Hwachon Dam, which the communists used to control the levels of the Fukhan and Han Rivers. Both rivers could be a threat to UN ground forces. In May, after numerous attempts using bombs and rockets had failed to destroy the dam, Douglas AD Skyraiders, assigned to VA-195 and VC-35 aboard the USS PRINCETON, made a torpedo attack which broke open the flood

The first MiG kill by an F-86 occurred on 17 December 1950, when four Sabres tangled with a flight of MiG-15s over Sinuiju and Lt Col Bruce Hinton scored the first 'kill.' This F-86A Sabre (49-1132) has probably not encountered any enemy aircraft, since it retains its drop tanks. These tanks were normally jettisoned when MiGs were sighted. F-86s were initially marked with white and black fuselage bands and a vertical black stripe on the tail to help distinguish them from the visually similar MiG-15. (USAF/NA)

gates and ended the threat against UN forces. The attacks were not limited to daylight hours; night missions by the B-26s, B-29s, F7Fs and F4Us kept up the pressure around the clock and placed a further strain on the enemy's ability to keep the frontline troops resupplied and equipped.

The near constant air attacks also made it difficult for the Chinese to build up enough strength to mount a massive general attack across the MLR. In conjunction with the attacks against enemy targets behind the MLR, fighter-bombers provided much needed air support along the front line when the communists tried to mount local offensives. In an attempt to coordinate the close air support, the Air Force set up the Joint Operations Center (JOC) which monitored all requests for air support. In theory a good idea, the main problem was the time between the request for support and how long it took to move up the chain of command to the JOC. In particular this system did not sit well with the Marines who felt their own system provided a faster response and better targeting information. Eventually a compromise was worked out — the Marines would still remain under JOC control, but stay in communication with Marine Tactical Air Control Squadron 2 (MTACS-2). MTACS-2 could assign a target requested by a Marine ground unit unless the JOC had another mission for them.

Battle For 'MiG Alley'

The air war up north also began to heat up during the spring of 1951. Chinese MiG-15s became bolder in their attacks, which gave the Sabres more opportunities to engage them. On 20 May several flights of F-86s tangled with a swarm of MiG-15s; when the engagement was over Captain James Jabara had scored a double kill making him the first jet ace in history.

During the summer, there was a marked change in the battles over 'MiG Alley.' The Sabre pilots increasingly found their latest opponents were more aggressive and better-trained than those engaged in earlier battles. These pilots, nicknamed 'honchos', were obviously not Chinese and when they were encountered the Sabres were in for a tough fight. Recently released documents from the Soviet Union confirm that many of these pilots were Russian aces from World War Two — all with extensive combat experience. Whole units from both the Soviet Union and other Soviet bloc nations were rotated through Korea to gain combat experience. Intelligence sources reported eyewitness accounts of MiG pilots with Caucasian features — information which tended to indicate that some of the MiGs were not being flown by Chinese or NKAF pilots. Only with the opening of the Soviet archives has this information finally been confirmed.

The introduction of Soviet pilots was the first step in the communist attempt to wrestle air control over northern Korea. Across the border, UN reconnaissance aircraft detected a massive buildup of MiG-15s and noted that there was a concerted effort to rebuild a number of airfields in the border areas to handle both jet and piston engine aircraft. These moves resulted in intensified attacks by the B-29s, which were tasked with the destruction of these bases along with other strategic targets. Inter-service cooperation sometimes led to Navy fighters being assigned to cover the B-29s such as on the raid to the railroad marshaling yards at Rashin. During this strike newly arrived F2H-2 Banshees from VF-172 aboard the USS ESSEX (CV-9) provided escorts for the lumbering B-29s. Much to the dismay of the Navy pilots, no MiGs showed up to test their new mounts.

The increase in the number of MiG encounters placed a great strain on the few F-86s flying with the 4th FIW while they escorted the B-29s. Often, the slower F-84s were assigned to escort duty along with the newly arrived Gloster Meteor Mk. 8s of the Australian No. 77 Squadron. No 77 Squadron had relinquished their F-51s in April. New units were also arriving to reinforce the expanded aerial campaign. The 27th FEW was relieved by the 136th FBW, an Air National Guard (ANG) unit, and the 49th FBW traded its F-80s for F-84s. Another Air National Guard unit, the 116th FBW, was sent to Japan in July. The increase in F-84 strength allowed an intensification of the attacks against enemy airfields, supply points, troop concentrations, and lines of communications. Even as these efforts increased, however, the MiGs became more aggressive. While UN losses were low, the mere appearance of the Russian-built jets often forced the fighter-bombers to jettison their ordnance in order to engage the MiGs. If this occurred the enemy had achieved his immediate goal — the target was spared until another day.

Despite the influx of jets, it was not all a jet war. F-51s were still shouldering a good share of the tactical bombing assignments, taking part in the largest air strike of the war to date on 9 May. The target was the air base at Sinuiju, which was hit by over 300 fighters from four USAF Wings. The F-51s carried out numerous missions over the north and, in some quarters, it was felt that the Mustangs were being used to attract the MiGs for the F-86s. Whether this was true or not the fighter-bombers were forced to deal with more and more attacks, often without the support of the F-86s, which were still limited by their numbers and range as to how large of an area they could cover. In late October it was

In addition to being the first jet war, Korea was also the first helicopter conflict. Helicopters were first used during the early days of the war to rescue downed pilots, and later, for casualty evacuation. This Sikorsky HO3S-1 Dragonfly, assigned to HU-1 aboard the PHILIPPINE SEA, rescues a pilot from the frigid waters of the Sea of Japan in early 1951. Speed was essential due to the low water temperature, which quickly caused hypothermia. (USN/NA)

RAAF F-51Ds taxi out for a mission loaded with rockets and napalm. The first Mustang (A68-729) survived the war and was scrapped in November of 1953. The next two F-51s were lost due to ground fire in March of 1951. Anti-aircraft fire took a heavy toll of allied Mustangs, whose liquid-cooled inline engines were more vulnerable to battle damage than aircraft powered by air-cooled radial engines. (USAF/NA)

finally decided to send additional F-86s from Air Defense Command (ADC) to replace the F-80s of the 51st FIW. The new commander of the wing was Colonel Francis Gabreski, the famed World War Two P-47 Thunderbolt ace. The unit's two squadrons, the 16th and 25th FIS, would fly out of Suwon.

When the summer turned to fall the air war along the Yalu increased in intensity. In particular the enemy airfields at Saamcham, Namsi, Chongchon, Uiji, and Taechon were the main targets for the B-29s, which tried to keep the communists from refurbishing them. The month of October proved to be the bloodiest month of the war for the B-29s. On 22 October the big bombers had been hit by a sudden MiG attack while bombing Taechon — one B-29 went down. The next day eight bombers headed for Namsi with a screening force of F-86s and a close escort of F-84s. Over one hundred MiGs hit the F-86s and they were unable to come to the aid of the bombers. The B-29s were hit by at least fifty MiGs, which brushed aside the F-84s and downed three of the Superforts. All the remaining aircraft were damaged and only three made it back to Okinawa. Over the next two days more B-29s were lost or damaged. The final tally for the month was five B-29s lost to fighters and flak and another eight heavily damaged. Additionally, seven F-86s, two F-84s, and a RF-80 had been lost. As a result of the heavy B-29 losses it was decided to withdraw them from future daylight bombing

missions. Encouraged by their success, the Chinese moved MiGs to the airfield at Uiji and piston engine attack aircraft to Sinuiju. The war had taken on a dangerous new dimension and air superiority over northern Korea was now in question.

Following the slaughter of the B-29s over Namsi the fighting over northern Korea intensified. Due to their superior numbers, the MiGs held the initiative north of Pyongyang — the Sabres were just too few in numbers to be everywhere. The fighter-bombers constantly encountered MiGs which had slipped past 4th FIW's patrols. Fortunately losses were few; the enemy flyers were often content to get the fighter-bombers to jettison their bomb loads. The F-86s continued to score and shot down fourteen MiGs during the early part of November. Then, on 18 November, a Sabre patrol spotted a dozen MiGs on the ground at Uiju Airfield, one of the few times that the Chinese tried to base their jets south of the Yalu. Two F-86s dropped down for a strafing attack and destroyed four MiGs and damaged several others. Nine days later four MiGs were downed during a sweep over 'MiG Alley.' The main event of the month came three days later on 30 November. The Chinese had become more brazen after the Namsi battle and had previously carried out a successful raid using Tu-2s against the South Korean held island of Taehwa-do, located off the mouth of the Yalu. The Chinese tried to repeat this success on 30 November with twelve Tu-2s covered by a

By early 1951, a sufficient number of South Korean pilots had been trained to fly F-51s. ROKAF pilots then began to fly missions along with their USAF instructors. These Mustangs, armed with rockets and 500 pound bombs, were flown by both US and ROK pilots. The closest F-51D carries the personal markings of Major Dean Hess, commander of the USAF instructor group working with the ROK Air Force. (USAF/NA)

mixed force of sixteen La-9s and the same number of MiG-15s. The strike force ran into thirty-one Sabres and, in the swirling dogfight which followed, eight Tu-2s, three La-9s, and a MiG-15 were shot down. The star of the day was Major George Davis, a World War Two ace who shot down the MiG and three of the bombers. These kills made Davis the fifth ace of the war and one of a select few pilots to become aces in both WW II and Korea. The battle might have become more interesting due to the presence of a large formation of Russian MiGs from the 196th Air Fighter Regiment. These MiGs had been spotted heading south by the Sabres at a much higher altitude, but had not engaged the F-86s. The ground controllers in Manchuria did not vector the Russian formation to help the Chinese and the MiGs proceeded southward without making contact. They returned to Manchuria in time to see the surviving Tu-2s stagger back from the slaughter at the hands of the F-86s. Like the Americans after the battle over Namsi, the Chinese realized the vulnerability of their piston engine bombers to jet fighters and never again committed their bombers in force south of the Yalu.

During this period the 51st Fighter Wing made the transition from F-80s to their new F-86Es and, by mid-December, both squadrons were fully operational. The addition of a new F-86 wing could not have come at a better time given the increase in air activity up north. The month started off badly for UN airmen when a flight of twelve Meteors from No. 77 Squadron were bounced by over forty MiGs while on a fighter sweep over 'MiG Alley' on 1 December. Although Flying Officer Bruce Gogerly destroyed one enemy aircraft, the MiG pilots shot down three of the Meteors. From this point on the Meteors were no longer used for fighter sweeps — it was recognized that they were inferior to the MiGs and were thereafter assigned to fighter-bomber work.

The F-86 pilots of the 4th and 51st FIWs quickly evened the score, downing at least twelve MiGs between 2 and 5 December. Two of these kills went to Major Davis who led the 'ace' race. On 13 December the 4th FIW encountered at least 145 MiGs during morning and afternoon fighter sweeps over Sinanju. The Sabres shot down thirteen MiGs — with Davis getting four, making him the first 'double ace' of the war. After this drubbing the Chinese chose to avoid combat and only three additional kills were registered during the rest of December.

Thus ended the first full year of air combat. Although the MiGs had inflicted some losses on the UN forces the F-86s had claimed 130 kills, 20 probables, and 144 aircraft damaged using a single wing of the Sabres. With another wing in place the future looked somewhat brighter than it had started out a year earlier when the Chinese had entered the conflict.

'SHOOT-YOU'RE FADED' (44-72278) runs up its engine after a check by the ground crew. This F-51D's rudder was replaced and is missing FORCE from the U.S. AIR FORCE title normally displayed over the serial number on its tail. This Mustang was transferred to the ROKAF in early 1953 when the USAF replaced the F-51Ds with F-86F Sabres. (USAF/NA)

Fighter-bombers occasionally flew so low over their targets, the blast from their bombs damaged or destroyed the attacking aircraft. Para-frags, fragmentation bombs fitted with small parachutes to slow them down, were first developed during World War II to allow the releasing aircraft to get far enough away from the blast. These para-frags have been dropped on a railroad bridge south of Pyongyang by a B-26 from the 452nd BW. (USAF/NA)

Fighter-bombers had to go in low to hit their targets and suffered the most losses of any type during the Korean War. This F-80C comes in for a bomb run on huts believed to contain camouflaged vehicles or supplies. Over the course of the conflict, the communists often set up decoy targets to catch the fighter-bombers in a flak trap. (USAF/NA)

An F9F-2B Panther (BuNo 123633), assigned to VF-191 from the USS PRINCETON (CV-37), flies over a valley in North Korea. Just above the river junction is a bridge which may be the Panther's target. Twenty-one mission markers are painted aft of the cockpit. The F9F is painted in overall Glossy Sea Blue (FS15042) – the standard color used for US Navy and Marine aircraft during the Korean War. (USN/NA)

Carrier operations are fraught with danger, even when flight operations are not in progress. An F4U-4B caught fire while parked forward aboard the USS PHILIPPINE SEA and had to be covered with chemical foam to prevent the fire spreading to other aircraft. The Corsairs were assigned to VF-113 and VF-114, while the Skyraiders belonged to VA-115. (USN/NA)

After their initial employment in the fighter and ground support roles, the F-82 Twin Mustangs were used for both night interdiction missions over North Korea and for night defense of Far East Air Force (FEAF) bases. These two F-82Gs were based at Kimpo Air Base (K-14) during the spring of 1951. (USAF/NA)

Britain's Royal Navy kept an aircraft carrier on station throughout the Korean War — alternating between the east and west sides of the peninsula. This Hawker Sea Fury from No. 801 Squadron prepares to launch from HMS GLORY in the summer of 1951. A Sea Fury FB Mk 11, flown by Lt Peter 'Hoagy' Carmichael of No. 802 Squadron from HMS OCEAN, shot down a MiG-15 in August of 1952. (USN/NA)

British and Australian Aircraft Carriers Deployed During the Korean War

HMS COLOSSUS
HMS WARRIOR
HMS THESEUS
HMS OCEAN
HMS TRIUMPH
HMS GLORY
HMAS SYDNEY

A Fairey Firefly Mk 5 lifts off from GLORY for a strike against targets around Wonsan. British carriers normally had one squadron of Sea Furies for escort duties and one squadron of Fireflys for attack missions. The standard Fleet Air Arm color scheme consisted of Extra Dark Sea Grey (FS16118) upper surfaces and Sky (FS14424) sides and under surfaces. British carrier aircraft wore alternating white and black identification bands around their fuselages and wings. (USN/NA)

(Above) The RAAF's No. 77 Squadron began to convert from F-51s to the Gloster Meteor F Mk 8 — a twin-engine, straight wing jet developed during World War II – in the spring of 1951. By the summer, the Australians were ready for combat and flew their first jet mission, escorting fighter-bombers near the Yalu, on 29 July. The Meteors were eventually found to be no match for the MiG-15s and they were switched to the fighter-bomber role. *Snookes* (A77-134) is being waved forward to its wheel chocks after a mission. (Horne via Australian War Memorial)

(Below) A pair of LT-6Gs from the 6147th Tactical Control Squadron (TCS) sit on the side of a runway awaiting their next mission. Smoke rockets mounted under the port wing of the near aircraft were used to mark targets for fighter-bombers. The LT-6G was a T-6G Texan trainer remanufactured for the FAC role in Korea. The Douglas C-47 Skytrain coming in for a landing is from the 21st Troop Carrier Squadron, the 'Kuyushu Gypsies.'(USAF/NA)

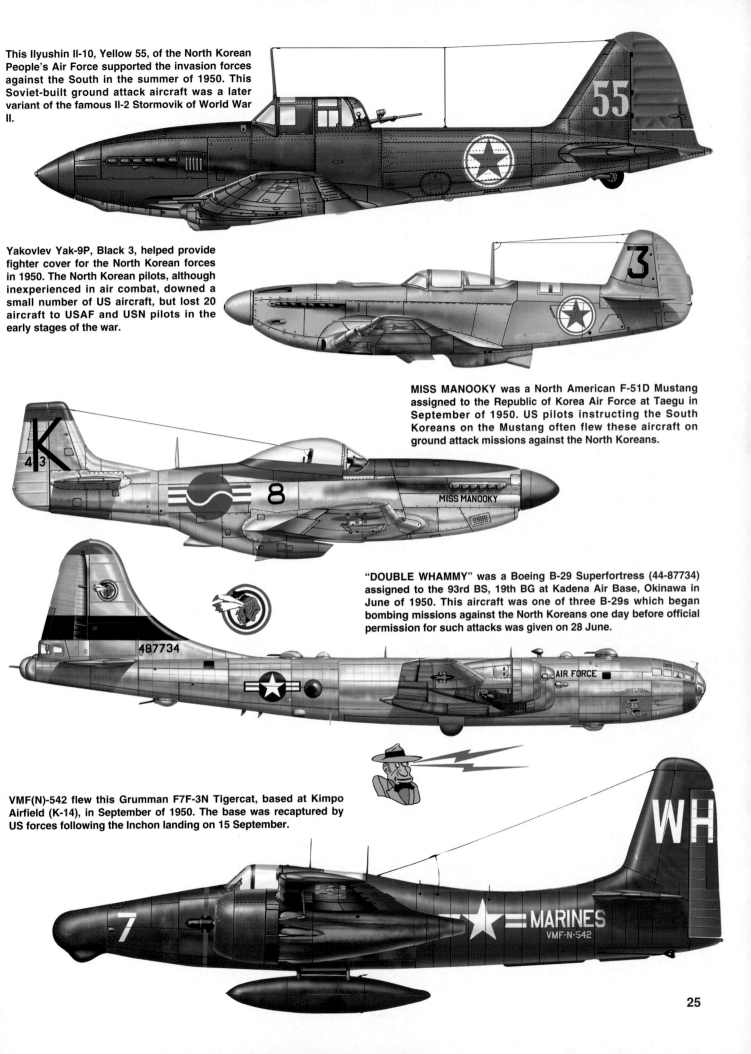

This Ilyushin Il-10, Yellow 55, of the North Korean People's Air Force supported the invasion forces against the South in the summer of 1950. This Soviet-built ground attack aircraft was a later variant of the famous Il-2 Stormovik of World War II.

Yakovlev Yak-9P, Black 3, helped provide fighter cover for the North Korean forces in 1950. The North Korean pilots, although inexperienced in air combat, downed a small number of US aircraft, but lost 20 aircraft to USAF and USN pilots in the early stages of the war.

MISS MANOOKY was a North American F-51D Mustang assigned to the Republic of Korea Air Force at Taegu in September of 1950. US pilots instructing the South Koreans on the Mustang often flew these aircraft on ground attack missions against the North Koreans.

"DOUBLE WHAMMY" was a Boeing B-29 Superfortress (44-87734) assigned to the 93rd BS, 19th BG at Kadena Air Base, Okinawa in June of 1950. This aircraft was one of three B-29s which began bombing missions against the North Koreans one day before official permission for such attacks was given on 28 June.

VMF(N)-542 flew this Grumman F7F-3N Tigercat, based at Kimpo Airfield (K-14), in September of 1950. The base was recaptured by US forces following the Inchon landing on 15 September.

25

An LT-6G from the 6147th TCS rolls right onto a target prior to marking it for fighter-bombers. The red panel across the wing made it easier for the fighter-bombers to spot the FAC. These FACs were nicknamed Mosquitoes after the radio call sign given to the unit. (USAF/NA)

A Marine HO3S-1 Dragonfly assigned to VMO-6 hovers over a forward airstrip north of Seoul. The Marines used the HO3S for casualty evacuation, rescue, and liaison. A rescue winch was mounted on the Dragonfly's roof. One 450 HP Pratt & Whitney R-985-AN-5 Wasp Junior engine powered the HO3S-1 to a maximum speed of 103 MPH (165.8 KMH). (USMC/NA)

The Bell HTL-4, which could carry more wounded then the HO3S, later replaced the Dragonfly in the casualty evacuation role with the US Marine Corps. Two wounded Marines are being placed on carrier racks mounted above the skids for transfer back to an aid station. WB on the aircraft's nose was the code for VMO-6. The HTL-4 was the Navy and Marine counterpart to the US Army's H-13D, which saw extensive service in the casualty evacuation role in Korea. (USMC/NA)

The Bell HTL-3 saw limited service in Korea, primarily in the liaison role. This aircraft was mainly deployed by the Navy and could carry two people; however, it was underpowered for use in the casualty evacuation role. The HTL-3 was fitted with a wheeled undercarriage and an enclosed tailboom, while the HTL-4 employed a skid landing gear and an open tailboom. (USN/NA)

A B-29 from the 98th BG flies over the rugged terrain of North Korea during a mission against a railroad marshaling area near the Yalu River. At this stage in the war, enemy fighters were not a serious threat to the B-29s, provided there was adequate fighter protection. The 98th BG was based at Yokota AB, Japan – headquarters of the Far East Air Forces Bomber Command – along with the 307th BG. The other three Superfortress groups – the 19th, 22nd, and 92nd – operated from Kadena AB, Okinawa. (USAF/NA)

This F-51D (44-64004) from the 18th FBG at Chinhae taxies through a small pond caused by runoff from a summer monsoon in September of 1951. The Mustang is fitted with 5 inch (12.7 CM) rockets and 500 lb (226.8 KG) bombs for a ground support mission. Weather conditions – ranging from snow and extreme cold in winter to hot and humid summers and rainstorms – played an important role in the air war. Airfields became inundated with water during the monsoons, creating all sorts of hazards for aircraft and their pilots. This Mustang was transferred to the ROKAF in October of 1951. (USAF/NA)

27

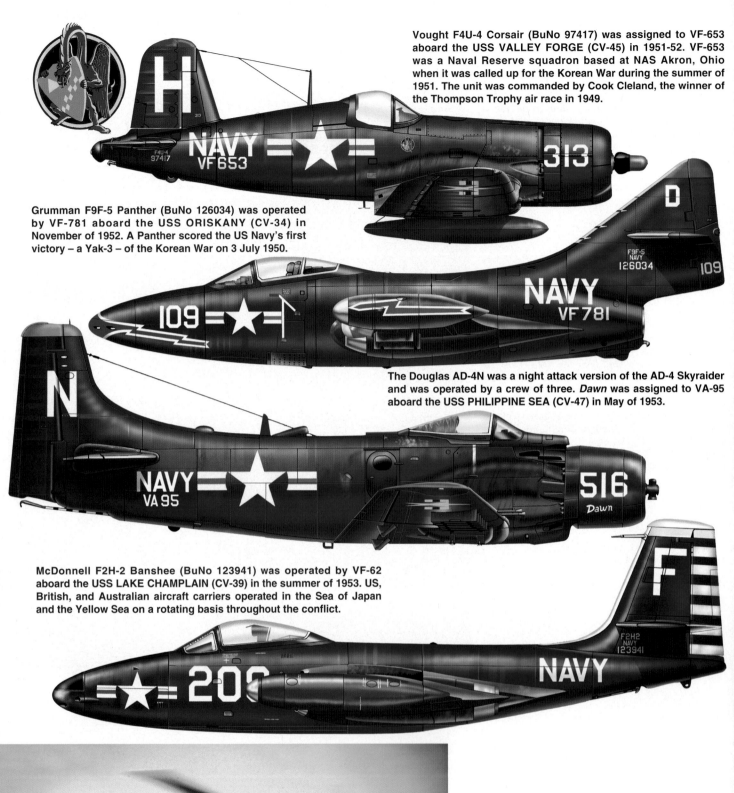

Vought F4U-4 Corsair (BuNo 97417) was assigned to VF-653 aboard the USS VALLEY FORGE (CV-45) in 1951-52. VF-653 was a Naval Reserve squadron based at NAS Akron, Ohio when it was called up for the Korean War during the summer of 1951. The unit was commanded by Cook Cleland, the winner of the Thompson Trophy air race in 1949.

Grumman F9F-5 Panther (BuNo 126034) was operated by VF-781 aboard the USS ORISKANY (CV-34) in November of 1952. A Panther scored the US Navy's first victory – a Yak-3 – of the Korean War on 3 July 1950.

The Douglas AD-4N was a night attack version of the AD-4 Skyraider and was operated by a crew of three. *Dawn* was assigned to VA-95 aboard the USS PHILIPPINE SEA (CV-47) in May of 1953.

McDonnell F2H-2 Banshee (BuNo 123941) was operated by VF-62 aboard the USS LAKE CHAMPLAIN (CV-39) in the summer of 1953. US, British, and Australian aircraft carriers operated in the Sea of Japan and the Yellow Sea on a rotating basis throughout the conflict.

An HO3S-1 Dragonfly assigned to HU-1 powers up on the deck of the USS ESSEX (CV-9). HU-1 provided detachments for all carriers deployed off the Korean coast during the war. The helicopters provided instant response for plane crashes and often made the difference between life and death for pilots forced down in the frigid waters. (Ivy)

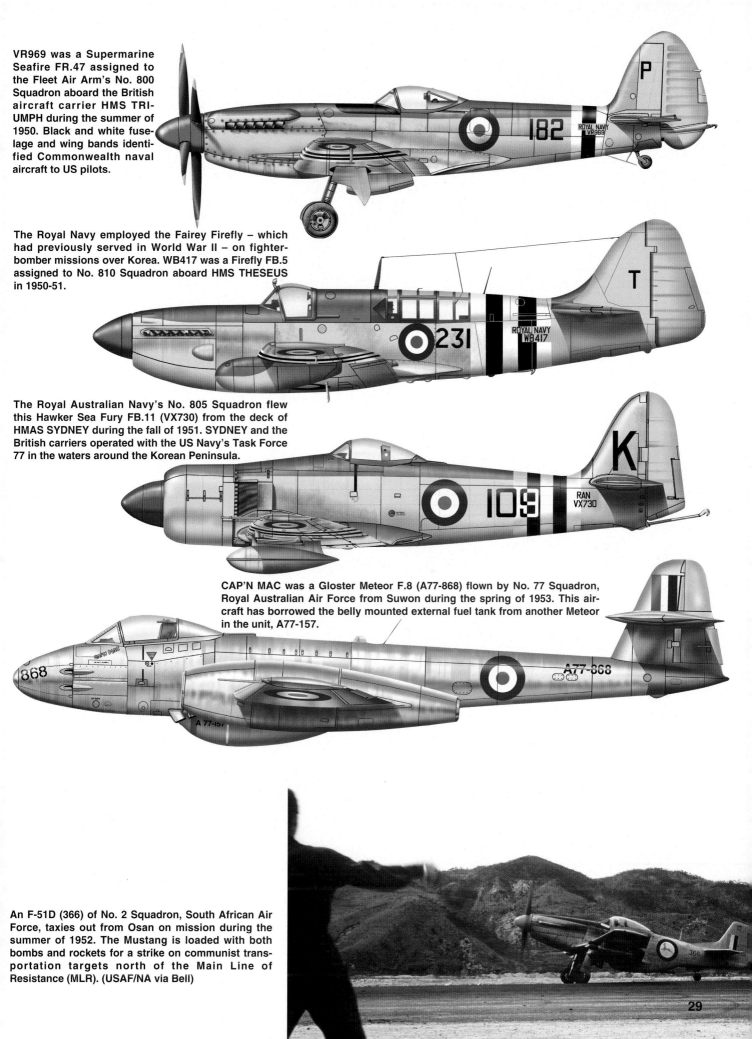

VR969 was a Supermarine Seafire FR.47 assigned to the Fleet Air Arm's No. 800 Squadron aboard the British aircraft carrier HMS TRIUMPH during the summer of 1950. Black and white fuselage and wing bands identified Commonwealth naval aircraft to US pilots.

The Royal Navy employed the Fairey Firefly – which had previously served in World War II – on fighter-bomber missions over Korea. WB417 was a Firefly FB.5 assigned to No. 810 Squadron aboard HMS THESEUS in 1950-51.

The Royal Australian Navy's No. 805 Squadron flew this Hawker Sea Fury FB.11 (VX730) from the deck of HMAS SYDNEY during the fall of 1951. SYDNEY and the British carriers operated with the US Navy's Task Force 77 in the waters around the Korean Peninsula.

CAP'N MAC was a Gloster Meteor F.8 (A77-868) flown by No. 77 Squadron, Royal Australian Air Force from Suwon during the spring of 1953. This aircraft has borrowed the belly mounted external fuel tank from another Meteor in the unit, A77-157.

An F-51D (366) of No. 2 Squadron, South African Air Force, taxies out from Osan on mission during the summer of 1952. The Mustang is loaded with both bombs and rockets for a strike on communist transportation targets north of the Main Line of Resistance (MLR). (USAF/NA via Bell)

29

Two 18th FBW Mustangs are loaded with rockets prior to a mission. The near F-51D (44-74488) wears the markings of the 35th FIW, which turned its F-51s over to the 18th when they moved back to Japan for transition back to F-80s. Additionally, the near F-51 is equipped with a cuffed Hamilton Standard propeller, while the far Mustang (44-74597) has an uncuffed Aero Products propeller. Both fighters were eventually transferred to the ROKAF. (USAF/NA)

The South African F-51 contingent was attached to the 18th FBW, flying joint operations with them throughout the war. This US-South African Mustang flight taxies past a stack of 500 lb bombs before reaching the runway for a mission. By this stage of the war, 18th FBW F-51s had been given a distinctive shark mouth on their noses. (USAF/NA)

RF-80As from the 67th Tactical Reconnaissance Wing (TRW) sit on the runway at Kimpo (K-14) waiting for a mission. Reconnaissance played a vital part in the aerial campaign, whether discerning enemy intentions, locating targets, or assessing bombing results. Korean carts and horses provide an interesting contrast to the marvels of jet aviation. (USAF/NA)

A 67th TRW RF-80A (45-8477) sits in the flooded parking area of Kimpo, while its pilot boards in preparation for the start of a mission. The Shooting Star was assigned to the Wing's 15th TRS and wore a green tail band. Even carrier aircraft had drier decks than this. (USAF/NA)

F-80s of the 51st Fighter Interceptor Wing (FIW) sit on the runway at Suwon (K-13) loaded with 500 lb bombs for a fighter-bomber sweep north of the Main Line of Resistance (MLR). Aircraft of the 51st carried a twin tail stripe and scalloped nose markings. The 16th Fighter Interceptor Squadron (FIS) used blue for their markings, while the 25th FIS wore red. The 51st FIW converted to F-86Es in the fall when the MiG menace became more dangerous. (USAF/NA)

Pilots flying north were comforted by the fact that if they were shot down, there was a chance of being rescued — either by helicopters, or if they came down at sea, by Grumman SA-16s of the 3rd Air Rescue Squadron (ARS). This SA-16A Albatross (49-080) gets a fresh water wash-down after plucking a downed pilot from the sea off western Korea. Saltwater corrosion was a major problem if the salt residue was not washed off. The 3rd ARS was based at Johnson AB, Japan when the war broke out, then transferred to bases in Korea to be closer to the action. (USAF/NA)

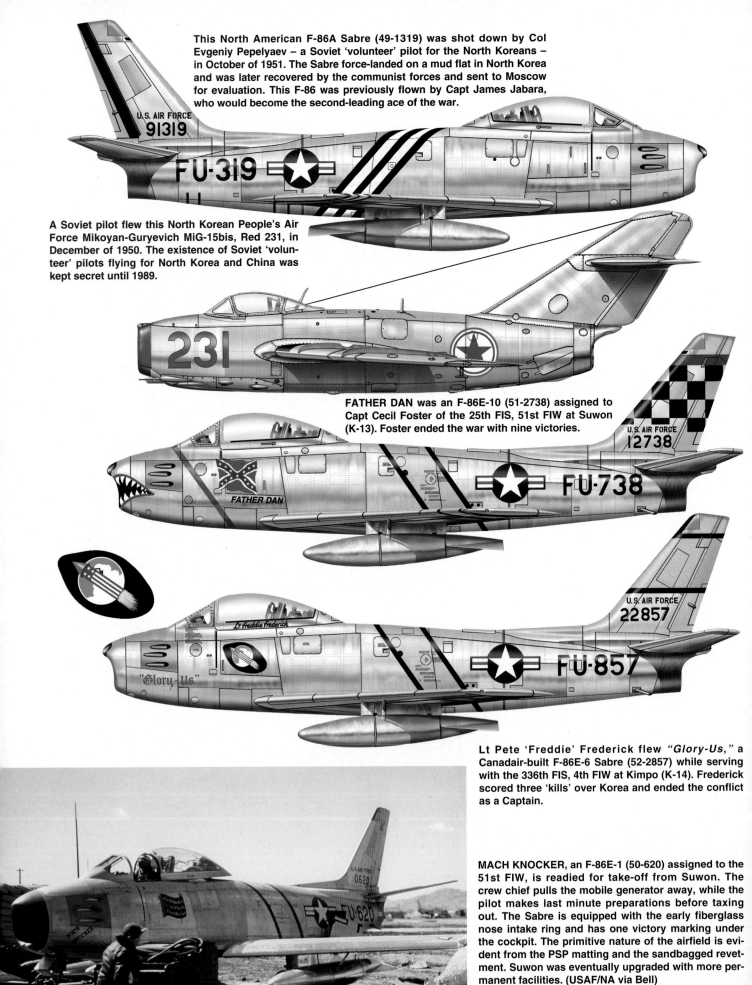

This North American F-86A Sabre (49-1319) was shot down by Col Evgeniy Pepelyaev – a Soviet 'volunteer' pilot for the North Koreans – in October of 1951. The Sabre force-landed on a mud flat in North Korea and was later recovered by the communist forces and sent to Moscow for evaluation. This F-86 was previously flown by Capt James Jabara, who would become the second-leading ace of the war.

A Soviet pilot flew this North Korean People's Air Force Mikoyan-Guryevich MiG-15bis, Red 231, in December of 1950. The existence of Soviet 'volunteer' pilots flying for North Korea and China was kept secret until 1989.

FATHER DAN was an F-86E-10 (51-2738) assigned to Capt Cecil Foster of the 25th FIS, 51st FIW at Suwon (K-13). Foster ended the war with nine victories.

Lt Pete 'Freddie' Frederick flew *"Glory-Us,"* a Canadair-built F-86E-6 Sabre (52-2857) while serving with the 336th FIS, 4th FIW at Kimpo (K-14). Frederick scored three 'kills' over Korea and ended the conflict as a Captain.

MACH KNOCKER, an F-86E-1 (50-620) assigned to the 51st FIW, is readied for take-off from Suwon. The crew chief pulls the mobile generator away, while the pilot makes last minute preparations before taxing out. The Sabre is equipped with the early fiberglass nose intake ring and has one victory marking under the cockpit. The primitive nature of the airfield is evident from the PSP matting and the sandbagged revetment. Suwon was eventually upgraded with more permanent facilities. (USAF/NA via Bell)

32

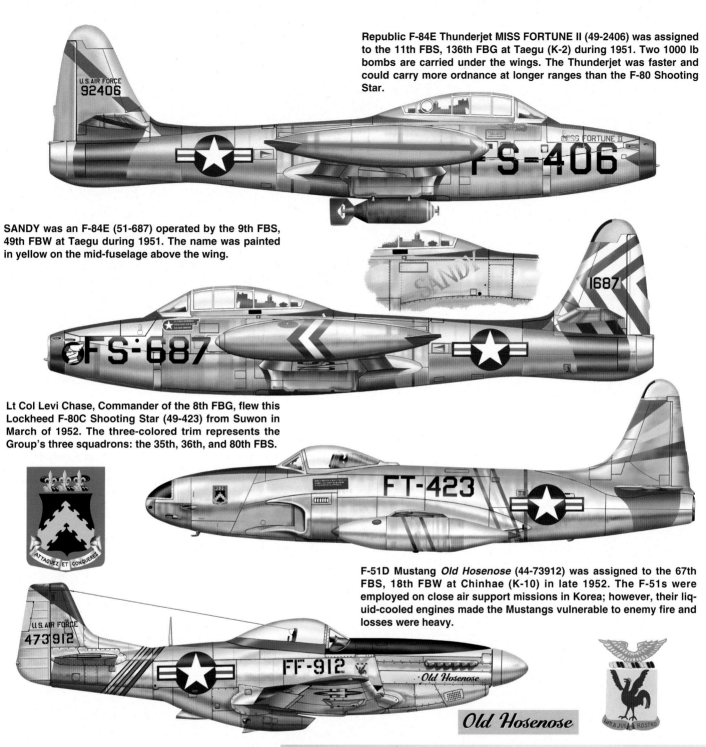

Republic F-84E Thunderjet MISS FORTUNE II (49-2406) was assigned to the 11th FBS, 136th FBG at Taegu (K-2) during 1951. Two 1000 lb bombs are carried under the wings. The Thunderjet was faster and could carry more ordnance at longer ranges than the F-80 Shooting Star.

SANDY was an F-84E (51-687) operated by the 9th FBS, 49th FBW at Taegu during 1951. The name was painted in yellow on the mid-fuselage above the wing.

Lt Col Levi Chase, Commander of the 8th FBG, flew this Lockheed F-80C Shooting Star (49-423) from Suwon in March of 1952. The three-colored trim represents the Group's three squadrons: the 35th, 36th, and 80th FBS.

F-51D Mustang *Old Hosenose* (44-73912) was assigned to the 67th FBS, 18th FBW at Chinhae (K-10) in late 1952. The F-51s were employed on close air support missions in Korea; however, their liquid-cooled engines made the Mustangs vulnerable to enemy fire and losses were heavy.

Frenchie/Lola K was an F-84E (51-613) assigned to the 8th FBS, 49th FBW at Taegu during 1952. The Thunderjet is loaded with bombs and a double layer of rockets for a strike against road traffic north of the front. The F-84 was the premier fighter-bomber of the war, replacing the F-80. Although no match for the MiG-15 at altitude, down on the deck the Thunderjet could hold its own against the faster Soviet fighter. F-84s claimed ten MiGs during the war. (USAF/NA via Bell)

33

When the war began, Boeing SB-17s were on station to escort B-29 flights over the ocean in case of problems. When the threat of MiGs arose, some SB-17s had their nose, top turret, and tail guns reinstalled. This aircraft comes in to land at Ashiya AB, Japan after dropping a life raft from under the fuselage to a downed B-29 crew over the Sea of Japan. An ASV (Air to Surface Vessel) radome is mounted under the nose in place of the chin turret. SB-17s were quickly replaced by SB-29s when MiGs grew in both strength and aggressiveness. (USAF/NA)

Two McDonnell F2H-2 Banshees assigned to VF-172 enter the landing circuit of the USS ESSEX (CV-9). The ESSEX arrived on station in June of 1951, bringing the new F2Hs with her into combat. The Banshees will circle to port and make their final approach from astern under the direction of the Landing Signal Officer (LSO). The ESSEX has just 'trapped' an F9F with its arresting gear. (USN/NA)

The ESSEX was shortly followed into the war zone by the USS ANTIETAM (CV-36). Arrayed along the ANTIETAMs after flight deck are aircraft from CVG (Carrier Air Group)-15: F4U Corsairs of VF-713, F9F Panthers assigned to VF-831 and VF-837, and a single AD-4W Skyraider from VC-11. All of CVG-15's fighter units were Reserve squadrons, called up in February of 1951 – after the intervention of the Chinese the previous November. (USN/NA)

More distinct variants of the Lockheed F-80 saw service in Korea than probably any other aircraft type, including the F-80, RF-80, F-94, and the T-33. This T-33A (49-970) from the 116th FBG undergoes maintenance in a revetment during the fall of 1951. These aircraft were used for general liaison duties or combat orientation flights for new pilots. Many T-33s were armed with two nose-mounted .50 caliber (12.7MM) machine guns in case MiGs were on the prowl. (USAF/NA)

An F-86A Sabre (49-1127) of the 4th FIW sits on the side of the runway at Kimpo, while a ground power unit is plugged into the Sabre's fuselage to provide the aircraft's systems with electrical power and compressed air. Behind the F-86, cargo specialists unload a Douglas C-124A Globemaster II (49-256). The C-124 was one the largest transports at the time and hauled large amounts of men and material to the war zone. Its clamshell nose doors allowed bulky cargo and vehicles to be loaded with relative ease. (USAF/NA)

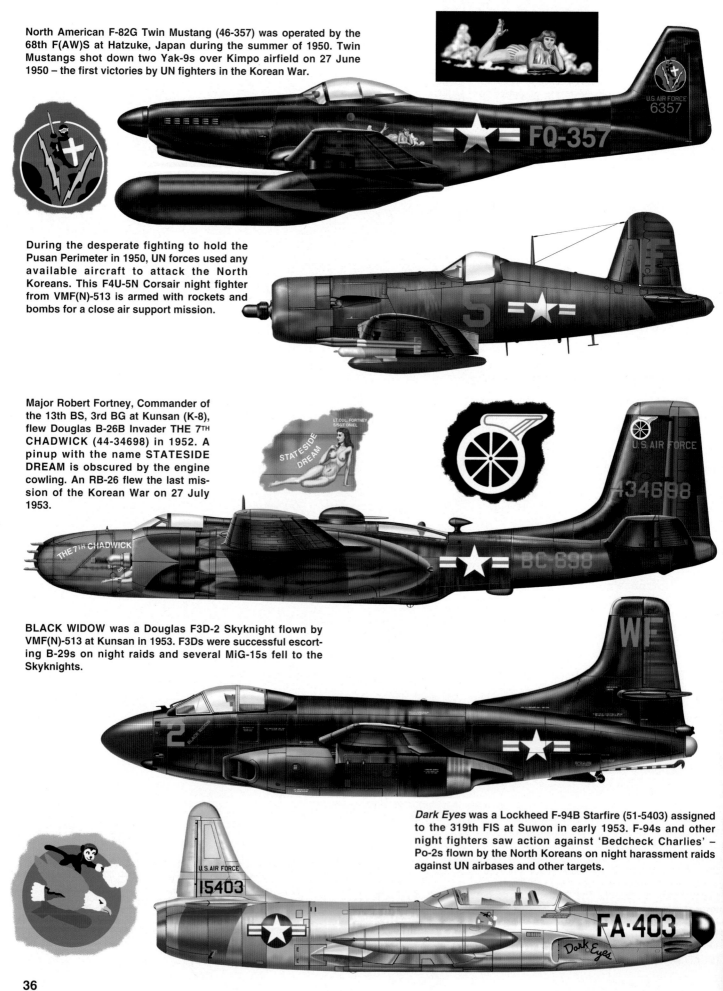

North American F-82G Twin Mustang (46-357) was operated by the 68th F(AW)S at Hatzuke, Japan during the summer of 1950. Twin Mustangs shot down two Yak-9s over Kimpo airfield on 27 June 1950 – the first victories by UN fighters in the Korean War.

During the desperate fighting to hold the Pusan Perimeter in 1950, UN forces used any available aircraft to attack the North Koreans. This F4U-5N Corsair night fighter from VMF(N)-513 is armed with rockets and bombs for a close air support mission.

Major Robert Fortney, Commander of the 13th BS, 3rd BG at Kunsan (K-8), flew Douglas B-26B Invader THE 7TH CHADWICK (44-34698) in 1952. A pinup with the name STATESIDE DREAM is obscured by the engine cowling. An RB-26 flew the last mission of the Korean War on 27 July 1953.

BLACK WIDOW was a Douglas F3D-2 Skyknight flown by VMF(N)-513 at Kunsan in 1953. F3Ds were successful escorting B-29s on night raids and several MiG-15s fell to the Skyknights.

Dark Eyes was a Lockheed F-94B Starfire (51-5403) assigned to the 319th FIS at Suwon in early 1953. F-94s and other night fighters saw action against 'Bedcheck Charlies' – Po-2s flown by the North Koreans on night harassment raids against UN airbases and other targets.

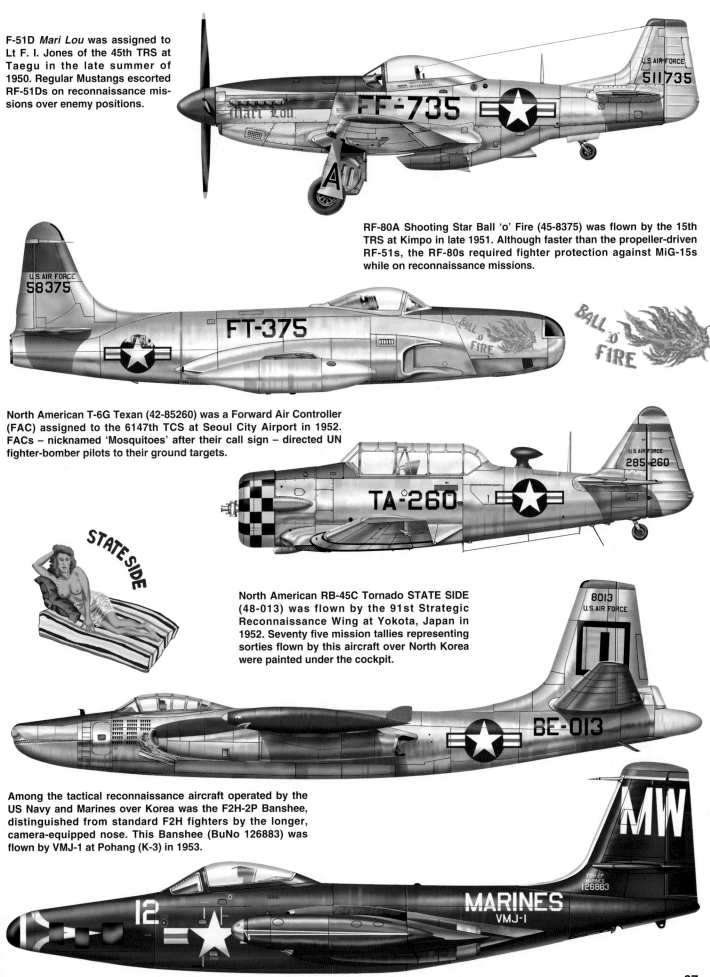

F-51D *Mari Lou* was assigned to Lt F. I. Jones of the 45th TRS at Taegu in the late summer of 1950. Regular Mustangs escorted RF-51Ds on reconnaissance missions over enemy positions.

RF-80A Shooting Star Ball 'o' Fire (45-8375) was flown by the 15th TRS at Kimpo in late 1951. Although faster than the propeller-driven RF-51s, the RF-80s required fighter protection against MiG-15s while on reconnaissance missions.

North American T-6G Texan (42-85260) was a Forward Air Controller (FAC) assigned to the 6147th TCS at Seoul City Airport in 1952. FACs – nicknamed 'Mosquitoes' after their call sign – directed UN fighter-bomber pilots to their ground targets.

North American RB-45C Tornado STATE SIDE (48-013) was flown by the 91st Strategic Reconnaissance Wing at Yokota, Japan in 1952. Seventy five mission tallies representing sorties flown by this aircraft over North Korea were painted under the cockpit.

Among the tactical reconnaissance aircraft operated by the US Navy and Marines over Korea was the F2H-2P Banshee, distinguished from standard F2H fighters by the longer, camera-equipped nose. This Banshee (BuNo 126883) was flown by VMJ-1 at Pohang (K-3) in 1953.

37

F-86As at Kimpo (K-14) are covered with camouflage netting for concealment against possible attack by enemy aircraft. Canvas covers protected the engine intakes from Foreign Object Damage (FOD) and the canopies from scratching. The closest Sabre was named *Gabby* and was flown by Colonel Francis Gabreski, the famous World War II ace who initially flew with the 4th FIW. He would later go on to command the 51st FIW when it re-equipped with F-86Es in late 1951. Although the danger of air attack always existed, the communists never mounted more than nighttime harassment attacks after 1950. (USAF/NA)

North American F-86 Sabre

Legendary World War II ace Colonel Francis 'Gabby' Gabreski flew in Korea with both the 4th and the 51st FIWs. He scored a total of six and a half kills: two with the 4th and the remainder with the 51st. These victories added to his 28 'kills' scored in Europe during World War II. Gabreski was one of just seven American pilots who became aces in both World War II and the Korean War. (USAF/NA)

On 23 October 1951, a force of eight B-29s was decimated by approximately 50 MiG-15s during a raid on Namsi airfield in northwestern North Korea. All of the Superfortresses were either shot down or suffered major damage. This B-29 crash-landed and was written off. The forward upper gun turret of the Superfortress was fitted with four .50 caliber machine guns, while the other three fuselage turrets and the tail turret each had two .50 caliber weapons. (Dunderdale)

A little over one month after the Namsi raid, the Sabre force got its revenge when it clobbered a Chinese bomber and fighter force. Major George Davis was the star of the day, downing three Tupolev Tu-2 bombers and a MiG-15. He describes his victories to Colonel Ben Preston (center) and Major Winton Marshall. Davis had just over two months to live; he was shot down and killed by a Soviet pilot over 'MiG Alley' on 10 February 1952, after having shot down two more MiGs during the melee. Davis was posthumously awarded the Congressional Medal of Honor. At the time of his death, George Davis was the top scoring Air Force ace with 14 kills. (USAF/NA)

Towards the end of 1951, the MiG-15s became more aggressive and the Chinese and North Koreans made plans to move aircraft from their sanctuaries across the Yalu into North Korea. The communists placed decoys around various airfields to deceive UN reconnaissance aircraft and lure fighter-bombers into flak traps. Although this decoy is an obvious fake, such a decoy could easily fool a pilot in a high-speed jet when dodging flak and looking out for MiGs overhead. (USAF/NA)

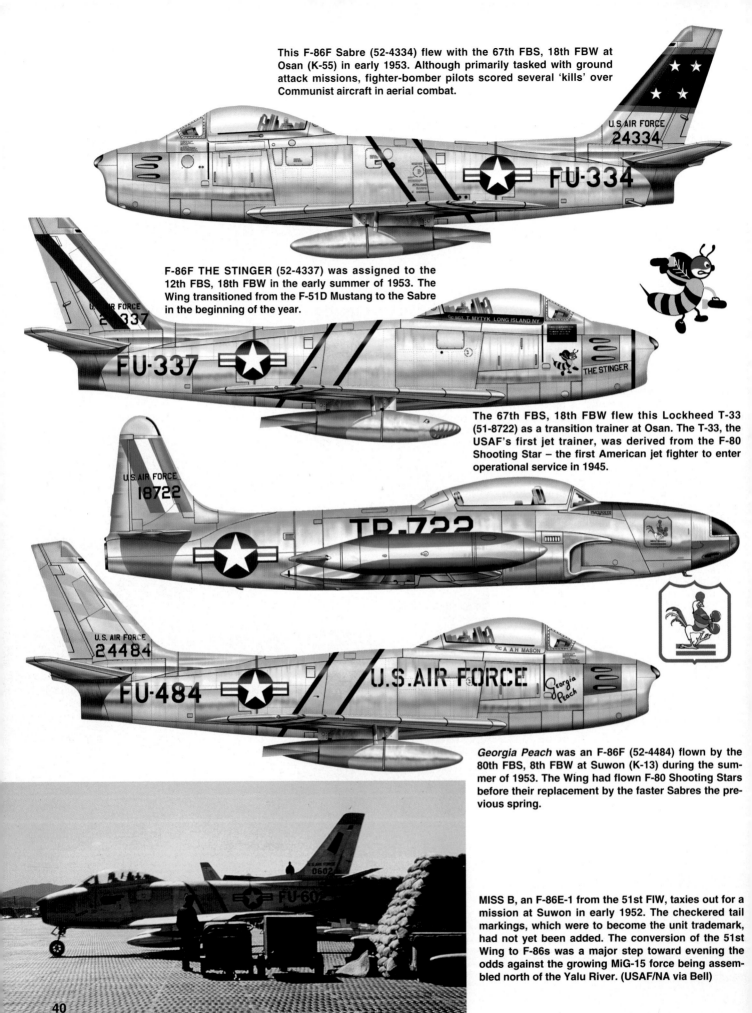

This F-86F Sabre (52-4334) flew with the 67th FBS, 18th FBW at Osan (K-55) in early 1953. Although primarily tasked with ground attack missions, fighter-bomber pilots scored several 'kills' over Communist aircraft in aerial combat.

F-86F THE STINGER (52-4337) was assigned to the 12th FBS, 18th FBW in the early summer of 1953. The Wing transitioned from the F-51D Mustang to the Sabre in the beginning of the year.

The 67th FBS, 18th FBW flew this Lockheed T-33 (51-8722) as a transition trainer at Osan. The T-33, the USAF's first jet trainer, was derived from the F-80 Shooting Star – the first American jet fighter to enter operational service in 1945.

Georgia Peach was an F-86F (52-4484) flown by the 80th FBS, 8th FBW at Suwon (K-13) during the summer of 1953. The Wing had flown F-80 Shooting Stars before their replacement by the faster Sabres the previous spring.

MISS B, an F-86E-1 from the 51st FIW, taxies out for a mission at Suwon in early 1952. The checkered tail markings, which were to become the unit trademark, had not yet been added. The conversion of the 51st Wing to F-86s was a major step toward evening the odds against the growing MiG-15 force being assembled north of the Yalu River. (USAF/NA via Bell)

40

1952

If 1951 ended on a good note, the beginning of 1952 started off badly. The 51st FIW lost seven F-86s during January, but in return claimed twenty-five kills. The 4th FIW, flying a mixture of F-86As and Es, was only able to knock down five MiGs. Maintenance problems arose due to a lack of parts — only half of the Sabres were available for operations. This hurt combat efficiency since the F-86 pilots were only able to get in about ten missions each during the month of January, not nearly enough to maintain their flying and combat skills. Added to this was a marked reluctance on the part of the enemy pilots to mix it up with F-86s after the losses they had taken in December. The material losses had been replaced and it was estimated that there were over 500 MiGs just across the Yalu at the Antung complex with additional units further north of the border.

February was a black month for the Sabre force. Although the 51st FIW's Major William T. Whisner became its first ace on 23 February, the 4th and 51st FIWs were only able to down seventeen MiGs between them. Whisner was another ace from WW II who joined the ranks of double aces in two wars. But his accomplishment was overshadowed by the loss of Major Davis on 10 February while flying cover for fighter-bombers attacking rail targets at Kunu-ri. Davis spotted a flight of a dozen MiGs ahead of his patrol and left the formation with his wingman to head them off. He managed to surprise the enemy formation and down two MiGs. In the process Davis lost his speed advantage and was in a precarious position. While Davis lined up a third MiG in his sights, a Russian pilot, Mikhail Averin, pulled into firing position behind Davis at 7 o'clock. Averin fired a short burst which hit Davis' F-86 just below the left side of the canopy. The F-86 went into an immediate spin and fell 32,000 feet (9753.6 м), crashing into the side of a mountain 30 miles (48.3 км) south of the Yalu. There was no parachute — in all probability Davis had been fatally injured by the MiG's cannon fire. For his heroic attack against such great odds Major George Davis was posthumously awarded the Congressional Medal of Honor. At the time of his death Davis had a total of eleven MiG and three TU-2 kills. Ironically, Davis was Averin's only victory during his tour over Korea.

Although maintenance was still a problem, March and April of 1952 were good months for the F-86s. The communist pilots were still aggressive and it cost them 39 MiGs in March and an additional 44 during April. This was due in part to the MiGs having to drop down to engage the fighter-bombers, which then opened them up to attacks by the Sabres. By June the enemy seemed to pull back from combat — there were few sightings and only 20 MiGs and three La-9s were claimed for the loss of four F-86s. On 23 June, one of the largest raids of the war took place, utilizing aircraft from the USAF, Navy, Marines, RAAF, and the ROKAF, against the hydro-electric complex at Suiho, approximately 30 miles (48.3 км) northeast of Antung. A force of 208 fighter-bombers covered by 108 F-86s hit the complex, the largest in Asia and the fourth largest in the world. For five days strikes were carried out, but the MiGs did not rise to the challenge. Over 1600 sorties were flown and only two Navy aircraft were lost, with both pilots being recovered. This series of attacks severely restricted power to many factories in the border areas and caused a significant drop in productions for several months. It was not until after the war that electric production was able to return to its prewar level.

Following these strikes another combined attack by UN forces, under the code-name Operation PRESSURE PUMP, was carried out against the North Korea capital at Pyongyang. Thirty high level targets were

selected and were hit on 11 and 12 July. Over 1200 sorties were flown during the two day period and all of the targets were either destroyed or severely damaged. In order to reduce civilian casualties warning leaflets were dropped a few days prior to the attacks in order to allow the population to leave the area. At the end of August, another attack was carried out and between the two series of strikes; Pyongyang was eliminated as a military threat for the remainder of the war. These attacks were part of a carefully escalating campaign on the part of the United Nations forces to influence the communist negotiators at the peace talks going on at Panmunjom. With the fighting stabilized along the front the only real pressure which could be applied was air power. Large scale and highly destructive air strikes against high profile targets were one way to get the enemy's attention; if enough pressure could be brought to bear it was hoped that negotiations would bring about meaningful results.

Interdiction

While the aerial battles over 'MiG Alley' continued, OPERATION STRANGLE was superseded by OPERATION SATURATE. SATURATE was to deal with the deficiencies which had been uncovered with STRANGLE. Instead of hitting a variety of points along the enemy's line of communication there would be a concentrated effort to stem the flow of men and material by hitting only specific segments of routes throughout the day. The strikes began in March, but were hindered by adverse weather. By late March, the effort began to achieve some results, but the overall impact on the enemy rail lines was not long lasting. The operation lasted through May, although inadequate numbers of serviceable aircraft handicapped Fifth Air Force. Prior to STRANGLE,

Helicopters came into their own in numerous areas during the Korean War, the most important being casualty evacuation. This Sikorsky HO3S-1 Dragonfly has landed with wounded on the fantail of the hospital ship USS CONSOLATION (AH-15). Hospital ships provided a modern, mobile casualty treatment center within easy access of the Korean coast and saved countless lives throughout the war. (USN/NA)

5th AF had suffered over 500 aircraft lost or severely damaged, but had only received 131 replacement aircraft. These included older F-84Ds, which had been upgraded, but were still not up to F-84E standards. Even when employing the aircraft of the 1st Marine Air Wing, STRANGLE could not be sustained; it gradually dwindled in scope while the air planners sought other ways to increase pressure against the North.

Part of the effort to increase the effectiveness of the fighter-bombers involved the use of in-flight refueling using modified B-29s and F-84s under Project HIGH TIDE. Pilots from the 116th FBW began training in this technique in late December of 1951 and by March of 1952 the unit was ready for combat. Other commitments forced postponement of trials, but on 28 May sixteen F-84s took off from Itazuki, Japan and were refueled over Taegu before hitting the industrial complex at Sariwon. Three more missions followed: another against Sariwon on 7 June, against Haeji on 22 June, and finally against Pyongyang on 4 July. All three missions involved refueling on the inbound flight, while the last strike also had the F-84s refueling on the way home. Although HIGH TIDE was successful and showed just how effective aerial refueling could be, the F-84's move to Korea eliminated the need for the refueling and the operation was terminated.

The Marines were also experimenting with a new technique known as Controlled Radar Bombing (CRB) for use at night or in inclement weather. This system, the MPQ-14 CRB, consisted of a generator power unit, a tracking radar, and a computer housed in a mobile ground unit. A ground controller in the unit monitored the aircraft under control and signaled when to drop the ordnance on the target. This system allowed close coordination between the controller, the pilot, and a forward observer on the ground. Results were excellent and the use of this system helped to stem the flow of men and material to the front-line and keep up round-the-clock pressure on the North.

Night Operations

While the main thrust of the air war seemed to concentrate on the aeri-

The escort carrier USS WINDHAM BAY (CVE-92) was pulled out of mothballs in 1950 and used as an aircraft transport throughout the war. She made ten trips to Korean waters carrying Navy, Marine, and Air Force aircraft above and below decks. On her deck are three Martin PBM Mariners, two AD Skyraiders, an F4U Corsair, and an F2H Banshee. During the conflict, a number of escort carriers made special trips to bring critically needed aircraft to the combat zone. (USN/NA)

al fighting over 'MiG Alley' and the daylight bombing raids, the air war did not stop when the sun went down. Night interdiction had begun early in the war and by 1952 had matured into a capable offensive tool. Both of the B-26 Invader units were utilized almost exclusively in night operations against enemy transportation targets, such as trains and trucks, in an effort to deny the communists the ability to build up their troop and supply levels along the front. Operating singly in the dark skies over North Korea, the Invaders stalked the main routes for trucks and trains coming south out of Manchuria. These missions were among the most dangerous types flown during the war due to enemy anti-aircraft fire, the mountainous terrain, and the horrendous weather conditions. Many B-26s simply disappeared, with no hint of their fate ever surfacing. Nevertheless, the crews achieved results which were well worth the effort involved. The Chinese and North Koreans could not move any appreciable amount of supplies by train or truck at night without suffering tremendous losses. This effort was costly in terms of crews and aircraft which were pushed to their limits. In-service strength varied due to maintenance problems which seemed to plague nearly every unit involved during the war, but both Invader units were able to operate at close to maximum efficiency due to the outstanding work of the ground crews. In May there was a paper shuffle when the 452nd BG was deactivated and returned to Air National Guard control. The 17th BG replaced the 452nd BG, but the original crews and aircraft remained in place.

Teaming up with the low flying Invaders were the F7F-3Ns and Corsairs of VMF(N)-513. Both units also carried night interdiction attacks north of the MLR. Operating in conjunction with C-47 or PB4Y flareships, the Marines carried out similar missions to those of the B-26 — with similar results. They also attempted to stop the nocturnal efforts of the North Koreans using piston engine aircraft to harass UN airfields, but with only limited success. In June Captain John Andre shot down a Yak-9 which combined with four kills from World War Two made him an ace, the first Marine to reach ace status in Korea.

During June the unit began to receive a new aircraft, the Douglas F3D Skyknight. The F3D was a portly, twin jet engine, straight winged night fighter. Twelve of these aircraft arrived at Kunsan in June and were assigned to fly escort for B-29s carrying out night missions along the Yalu. The B-29s had been relegated to the night bombing role after the debacle over Namsi. To help locate their targets in the dark, the B-29's used Short-Range Navigational Radar (SHORAN). SHORAN consisted of two radar beams which guided the B-29s to their targets. The bombers flew along the track of one beam and at the target the other beam intersected it. When this point was reached the bombers simply

The ability of Task Force 77 to use replenishment ships off the coast allowed the aircraft carriers to remain on station for longer periods of time — giving great flexibility in their deployment. The BON HOMME RICHARD (CV-31) and destroyer UHLMANN (DD-687) take on fuel from the oiler GUADALUPE (AO-32). The UHLMANN was the last FLETCHER class destroyer to see service in the US Navy, being retired in 1972. (USN/NA)

dropped their bombs with fairly accurate results. The concept was a further development of the German night bombing techniques pioneered during the Battle of Britain in 1940. Initially the communists were able to offer little opposition to the night raiders except for anti-aircraft fire. By late 1952, however, the B-29s were being intercepted by enemy night fighters. The Marines started flying escort for the bombers shortly after their arrival in Korea, although the small number of F3Ds limited their effectiveness. Newly arrived Skyknights and crews were gradually made operational and the additional Marine aircraft began to score. Their first victory occurred on 2 November when Major William Stratton and Master Sergeant Hans Hoglind downed an elderly Yak-15 jet fighter. Five nights later, Captain O.R. Davis downed a MiG-15, the first one claimed for the squadron. The unit flew both barrier patrols ahead of the bomber formations and close escort for the B-29s. The Marines were joined in November by F-94s of the 319th FIS when the restrictions on them operating north of the MLR were lifted. This coordinated effort helped to keep pressure on the enemy supply lines, bridges, airfields, and industrial targets. Coupled with the interdiction efforts of the B-26s and the Marines, the Chinese and North Koreans were severely hampered in their attempts to keep supplies flowing to the front. Although air power alone was never able to completely shut down the flow of supplies, without it the ground war would have been far more difficult and costly to wage.

Sea Support

Off the Korean coast, the UN fleet (primarily consisting of US Navy units) roamed up and down the peninsula, striking at targets of opportunity. The ability to replenish at sea gave the carriers a great deal of flexibility and staying power. Efforts combined with other UN forces allowed missions to be carried out which severely hurt the communists, such as the Suiho strikes and PRESSURE PLATE. During the summer of 1952 the Navy also began using a new weapon, the remote-controlled F6F-K Hellcat drone, against hard targets in North Korea. Guided by an AD Skyraider mother ship, six missions were flown using the drones from Guided Missile Unit 90 aboard the USS BOXER during the remainder of the year.

Weapons such as Hellcat drones were the exception to the rule; Navy pilots carried out thousands of conventional strikes along and above the MLR. The largest strike of the war by naval aviation occurred on 1 September when aircraft from the USS ESSEX, PRINCETON, and

The Korean weather was atrocious in the winter and greatly increased flying hazards. A ground crew sweeps snow off the upper surfaces of a B-26C assigned to the 3rd BW at Kunsan (K-8) in February of 1952. Tarpaulins were often placed over canopies and control surfaces of aircraft parked outdoors to protect them against ice damage. (USAF/NA)

Maintenance was even harder during the harsh Korean winters. This 3rd BW B-26B (44-34542) has been pulled into canvas shelters to allow the ground crew to work on the engines under some cover from the elements. Despite such conditions, the Invaders were constantly on the prowl at night over enemy supply lines in an attempt to stem the flow of men and materiel to the front lines. (USAF/NA)

this was the opening round in an escalation of the fighting by the Russians. Fortunately, the Russians never intervened. For a few hours on 18 November, however, the vision of the possible start of World War Three flashed through the minds of American military leaders. After the attack all mention of it was classified ' Top Secret" and it was not until years later that the story was released to the press.

BON HOMME RICHARD laid waste to the synthetic oil refinery at Aoji. Further south, naval airmen supported the 1st Marine Division with direct attacks along the front and against supply lines to the rear of the MLR. These strikes cost the Chinese thousands of troops and much needed supplies and helped the leathernecks on the ground to retain their positions.

In response to this support, the Chinese tried to stop the fighter-bombers with occasional MiG sorties, similar to what they had tried to do further north against the F-51s, F-80s, and F-84s. In one incident a Marine F4U-4B Corsair, flown by Captain Jesse Folmar, shot down a MiG-15 which tried to turn with the more maneuverable, albeit slower, piston engine fighter. Folmar's Corsair was then damaged by other MiGs, which forced him to bail out. He was subsequently rescued by an Air Force SA-16 Albatross. Encounters with MiGs were not typical, but on 18 November F9F-5 Panthers from the USS ORISKANY (CVA-34) were vectored toward a flight of unidentified aircraft approaching the task force from the vicinity of Vladivostok. The aircraft turned out to be Russian MiG-15s, which suddenly bounced the Panthers over international waters. In the ensuing dogfight two of the MiGs were shot down and another damaged before the engagement broke up. One Panther was damaged, but managed to make it back to the carrier. Twice more during the day fighters were vectored out to intercept suspicious flights, and in one case, MiGs were again sighted, but no contact occurred. Taped intercepts of Russian transmissions made during the battle made it clear that this was a deliberate attack and for a time it was feared that

More F-86s

During July of 1952, the 4th FIW relinquished its older F-86As for newer F-86Es. Nine of the F-86As were converted to reconnaissance aircraft under Project ASHTRAY. Their armament was removed and two K-9 cameras were mounted horizontally in the gun compartment. A few retained a pair of machineguns for self-defense, but firing them caused the cameras to shake which resulted in blurry pictures; their use was not encouraged unless absolutely necessary. (Three F-86Fs were also converted to the same configuration under Project HAYMAKER later in 1953.) These reconnaissance Sabres provided a more effective platform for work over North Korea than the RF-80s then in service. The RF-86As were better able to escape patrolling MiGs due to their greater speed and maneuverability.

While the 4th FIW was getting their new Sabres, the 51st FIW received a third squadron to round out its strength. The 39th FS had been flying F-51s with the 18th FBW, but when the number of Mustangs dwindled, the unit was re-equipped with F-86s. At the same time an even newer version of the F-86 began to reach units in Korea. This was the F-86F, which featured an improved wing and engine. This finally gave the Air Force pilots a fighter which was superior to the MiG-15 in all but altitude capability. F-86Fs began to see action during the late summer and their pilots began scoring kills almost immediately. The qualitative and quantitative improvements to the fighter force occurred at the same time as the aerial battles up north took an upswing.

An LT-6G Mosquito (49-3573) flies low over mountainous terrain in search of ground targets. The Forward Air Controllers (FACs) were usually assigned to a specific area, a practice which allowed the pilot to become familiar with the terrain. This made it easier to spot anything suspicious which was not there the day before. Mosquito pilots called in fighter-bombers after marking the targets with white phosphorous rockets mounted beneath the LT-6G's wings. (USAF/NA)

Three Lockheed F-80 Shooting Stars from the 8th FBG at Suwon (K-13) await a call from a FAC to hit an enemy target. Loaded with 500 lb (226.8 KG) bombs, the fighter-bombers stayed on station until they either received a call or reached 'Bingo' fuel — the point where they have just enough fuel to get home with a few minutes' reserve. Lacking a FAC call, fighter-bombers often looked for targets of opportunity rather than land with a full load of ordnance. (USAF/NA)

The MiGs became more aggressive and intent on action. On 9 September, during a raid on the North Korean Military Academy, 175 MiGs intercepted a strike by 82 F84s, which was covered by a heavy force of F-86s. Despite heroic efforts on the part of the F-86s, 77 MiGs broke through and downed three F-84s while forcing others to jettison their bomb loads. At least six MiGs were shot down and six more were claimed as probables. Throughout the remainder of the year the communists kept up the pressure, but the F-86 pilots held their own and soundly defeated the MiGs at every turn. By the end of the year, there were sixteen new aces between the two fighter wings — ten from the 4th and six from the 51st.

The 4th FIW had also flown a number of missions to see how well the Sabre performed in the fighter-bomber role. Attacks were carried out against Sinuiju and Uiji airfields and the railroad marshaling yards at Kunu-ri. Results were good, but over Kunu-ri, the unit lost its commander, Colonel Walker (Bud) Mahurin, the famous WW II ace who was downed by ground fire and captured by the Chinese. Mahurin, who had three and a half kills, was subjected to a lengthy imprisonment and 'brainwashing' by the Chinese; he was not released until well after the war. His book on this experience, "Honest John", describes in vivid detail his treatment at the hands of the communists and foreshadowed the future experiences of American pilots during the Vietnam War. As a result of the 4th FIW's work, plans were made to reequip both the 8th and 18th FBWs with F-86Fs as new production fighters became available. Included in the conversion plan was No. 2 Squadron of the South African Air Force, then attached to the 18th FBW. This change would give the fighter-bomber units the flexibility to be used in their primary mission of ground support and to supplement the fighters in the battles over 'MiG Alley.' Initial projections for the changeover were for November, but a variety of problems pushed this back and actual operations with the new aircraft did not begin until 1953.

This FAC LT-6G was hit by enemy fire, yet was fortunate to make it back to friendly territory. The amount of damage made it likely this aircraft was salvageable and would fly again. FACs were hated by enemy ground troops and, if shot down and captured, were often subjected to horrible torture before being killed. Every effort was made to rescue any FAC shot down behind enemy lines. (USAF/NA)

A group of 8th FBG F-80s armed with 1000 lb (453.6 KG) bombs taxi down an access ramp at Suwon. These weapons were used with good effect against railroad lines since even a near miss could cause a great deal of damage against the rail bed. Unfortunately, operating on Pierced Steel Planking (PSP) runways caused a great deal of damage to tires and blowouts often occurred when taking off — an unpleasant event when loaded with fuel and ordnance. (USAF/NA)

While the fighter-bombers kept up pressure against enemy ground targets, the Sabres continued to take on the MiG-15s over 'MiG Alley.' This F-86E (51-2790) from the 25th FIS, 51st FIW has just jettisoned its 120 gallon (454.2 L) drop tanks after sighting Chinese fighters. These Japanese-made tanks, unlike US manufactured tanks, tended to ride up over the tops of the wings when released. This caused damage to the wing leading edges if the pilots were not careful. Japanese-made tanks were normally painted Olive Drab (FS34087), while the US-made tanks were silver. The color difference made the Sabre pilots aware of which type they were carrying. (USAF/NA)

One of the young pilots flying north to 'MiG Alley' was Lt Virgil 'Gus' Grissom, who flew 100 missions during his tour in Korea. He later became one of the original Mercury Seven Astronauts. Two other Mercury astronauts, John Glenn and Wally Schirra, also flew in Korea with Glenn downing three MiGs and Schirra getting one. (USAF/NA)

MiG-15 (Fagot)

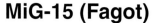

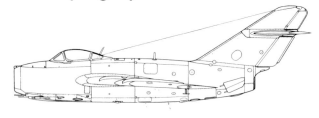

A MiG-15 goes down under the guns of Lt Robert Sands, who flew F-86s for the 16th FIS, 51st FIW. This was one of Sands' three 'kills' during the war. The MiG-15's landing gear has extended due to system failure caused by battle damage. The Sabre's six .50 caliber (12.7MM) machine guns were often criticized by American pilots for their lack of punch against the Soviet-built fighters; it often took hundreds of rounds to bring a MiG down. On the other hand, only a few hits from the MiG-15's three slow firing cannons – two 23MM and one 37MM – were enough to bring down an F-86 or fighter-bomber. (USAF/NA)

During the summer of 1952 the 136th FBW – an Air National Guard unit called up at the beginning of the conflict – was redesignated the 58th FBW. To bring all the F-84 Thunderjet units up to strength, enough F-84Gs were shipped to Korea so that by September all the fighter-bomber wings were at full strength — the first time this had occurred in over a year. The markings on the nose and tip tanks were yellow with black outlines. (USAF/NA)

There were a multitude of other tasks for which aircraft were utilized in Korea — aside from bombing and fighter sweeps. The new de Havilland Canada L-20 Beaver was used for communication, casualty evacuation, supply, and a host of other jobs. This Beaver from the 10th Liaison Squadron takes off from a small forward airstrip after delivering supplies and personnel to the forward area. Docile and easy to fly, the L-20 was an ideal aircraft for getting in and out of short fields with little difficulty. (USAF/NA)

A C-47A (42-108993) is loaded with wounded from an ambulance at a small forward airstrip near the front line. After being stabilized at a MASH (Mobile Surgical Army Hospital) unit or forward aid station, casualties were then flown to better equipped rear area facilities for additional medical attention. The overall mortality rate for wounded dropped dramatically compared to the rate for World War II. (USAF/NA)

47

One of the best morale boosters was mail from home. This Stinson L-5E Sentinel (44-17609) drops a mail sack to troops manning an M-19 40MM self-propelled anti-aircraft vehicle. L-5s were used throughout the war for communications and liaison. Early in the war, Sentinels were also used as FACs until replaced by faster T-6s. (USAF/NA)

A Lockheed P2V-5 Neptune assigned to VP-1 heads out on a patrol mission from Atsugi, Japan. Navy patrol squadrons – flying coastal surveillance and reconnaissance, anti-submarine patrols, convoy escort, gunfire spotting, and interdiction missions – performed one of the most unheralded jobs of the war. A number of these aircraft were downed over international waters by Soviet and Chinese fighters during the war. Seven Neptune squadrons eventually saw service in Korean waters during the conflict. (USAF/NA)

One of the stalwarts of the US Navy's Korean War effort was the aircraft carrier USS BOXER (CV-21), which took part in four deployments. She also delivered the initial load of 145 P-51s to Korea in July of 1950. The BOXER carries a mixed load of Skyraiders, Panthers, and a lone Banshee spotted adjacent to the island. Leading the starboard column of aircraft, on the forward edge of the flight deck, is an AD-4W. This airborne early warning variant of the AD Skyraider is distinguished by its large under fuselage radome. The carrier's bow mounted 40MM guns have their barrels removed. (USN/NA)

48

An F9F-2 assigned to VF-721 is launched off the port catapult of the USS KEARSARGE (CVA-33). VF-721 was a Reserve unit from NAS Glenview, Illinois, which had served earlier on the BOXER. The canopy is kept open during a launch for easy escape in case the aircraft or catapult looses power and the Panther goes into the water. The last digit of the aircraft's code number (104) is repeated on the vertical fin aft of the air wing code letter. (USN/NA)

F4U-4 Corsairs of VF-192 and 193 aboard the USS PRINCETON (CV-37) warm up their engines prior to taxing forward for launch. These aircraft are armed with 500 lb bombs under the wings. Corsairs formed the backbone of Navy and Marine carrier attack squadrons during most of the war. Of the 564 Navy and Marine Corps aircraft lost during the conflict, 312 were F4Us. (USN/NA)

This F4U-4 of VF-884 suffered ground fire damage to its main landing gear during a strike against Wonsan in late 1952, forcing it to belly in onboard the KEARSARGE. The tail wheel is down and the hook may have already snagged the first arresting wire. This Corsair made it with little damage and was later repaired to fight again. The four stubs under each wing were pylons for mounting bombs or rockets. (USN/NA)

The Marines experimented with helicopters for mass troop and supply movement, a forerunner of airmobile operations later used in Vietnam. These Sikorsky HRS-1s of HMR-161 depart from the USS SICILY (CVE-118) to deploy a battalion of Marines near Inchon. Each HRS could carry eight fully equipped troops in and out of battle. The Sikorsky HRS was called the H-19 Chickasaw by the US Army and Air Force, who also operated the type in Korea. (USMC/NA)

A fully equipped Marine fire team exits a HRS-1 on the beach during OPERATION MARLIN 5 in September of 1952. This exercise successfully tested the concept of moving supplies and personnel by helicopter from an aircraft carrier offshore to the coast. The Marines eventually tested this vertical envelopment concept in battle and moved an entire unit and its artillery behind enemy lines with remarkable success. During the Korean War, Marine helicopters were painted overall Glossy Sea Blue (FS15042) with white lettering. (USMC/NA)

During hot weather, the F-84s often used Jet Assisted Take Off (JATO) bottles to help get the heavily loaded fighter-bombers into the air. This F-84E Thunderjet (51-634) from the 49th FBG uses a single JATO bottle to help it lift off the runway at Taegu (K-2). The aircraft is armed with two 500 lb bombs under the wings. (USAF/NA)

50

The 452nd BG was transferred back to Air National Guard control in the spring of 1952; however, its men and aircraft remained in Korea under a new name — the 17th BG. The two B-26 groups each took half of Korea as their responsibility, the 3rd BG at Kunsan (K-8) operating over western Korea and the 17th BG at Pusan (K-9) flying over the east. This B-26C Invader (44-34656) has just returned to Pusan from a mission against rail targets. The B-26 is taxiing in front of a Marine Douglas R5D — the Navy and Marine designation for the C-54. (USAF/NA)

An F2H-2 Banshee of VF-11 from the USS KEARSARGE rolls in on a target over North Korea in November of 1952. The VF-11 insignia is painted below the windshield. The leading edges of the wings and tail and the jet exhaust areas are natural metal, while the top of the vertical stabilizer is Light Blue (FS15102). The Banshee proved to be an effective and stable fighter-bomber and was well liked by its pilots. The first major success of the McDonnell firm, the F2H Banshee paved the way for one of the greatest fighters in aviation history — the F-4 Phantom. (USN/NA)

51

(Above) Fairchild C-119 Flying Boxcars of the 314th Troop Carrier Group (TCG) carry elements of the 187th Airborne Regiment to Korea in late 1952. The C-119s were ideal for airborne operations, yet the situation in Korea did not lend itself to airborne drops after the early months of the war. The 187th Abn Rgt was kept as a theater reserve and was flown to Korea on numerous occasions when a large-scale communist offensive seemed imminent. (USAF/NA)

(Below) An F-86F (51-12948) assigned to the 335th FIS, 4th FIW is readied for a mission from Kimpo north to 'MiG Alley' in December of 1952. The use of tarps to protect the canopy, control surfaces, and leading edge of the wing was necessary during the harsh winter climate. The reinforced ammunition bin door formed part of the means of access to the wing and cockpit. A 120 gallon (454.2 L) drop tank is mounted under each wing to increase the Sabre's endurance. (USAF/NA)

1953

By the beginning of 1953, the Korean War had been raging for two and a half years — with no end in sight. The front line had remained relatively stable since June of 1951 with only local action causing minor shifts. Nevertheless, it had been a costly time in men and material for both sides. The peace talks had broken down the previous November over the question of prisoner repatriation and both sides had left the conference table. Since the United Nations had decided not to resume a full-scale ground offensive to force the communists back to the negotiations table, the weapon with which to bring continued pressure on the North was air power.

The arrival of more F-86Fs gave the fighter wings a marked advantage over their MiG counterparts. The transition of the 8th and 18th FBWs to the new jets also increased the total number of fighters available should the north pull out all the stops in an attempt to wrestle air superiority from the Sabres. The 18th flew its first mission with their new mounts at the end of February, while the 8th did not use theirs in combat until early April. It took a while to make the complete transition for both units, but by early June both wings had completed the changeover and were flying north looking for both ground targets and MiGs. This transition marked both the F-51 Mustang's and F-80's end of service in Korea, although the ROKAF continued to use the Mustang for the remainder of the war. The last ROKAF F-51 was not retired until 1957.

The 4th and 51st FIWs continued their decimation of the MiG-15 force. Since the F-86 had arrived two years earlier, twenty-three Sabre pilots had become aces. Over the next seven months an additional sixteen pilots would achieve that status, including the top American ace of the war, Captain Joseph McConnell. The odds facing them were daunting. North of the Yalu were nearly 1000 MiGs and 100 IL-28s, a new twin-engine jet bomber, and over 400 other conventionally powered fighters and bombers. Included in this force were some MiGs fitted for night fighting; these had already begun to hit the night flying B-29s. To counter the night-fighting MiGs presence, the Marines F3Ds, in concert with USAF F-94s, had begun escort operations in late 1952. During January the Marines knocked down three MiGs, putting a damper on the enemy's night attacks. This, along with the barrier patrols flown by the F-94s along the Yalu, allowed the B-29s to finish out the war without taking heavy losses.

The Ace Race

When the fighting picked up over 'MiG Alley' the scores of individual pilots began to climb. Some pilots ignored orders not to cross the Yalu and chased enemy aircraft into Manchuria, particularly members of the 16th FIS. When this became known to higher authorities, all hell broke loose — the squadron was ordered to stand down for a few days while the wing CO read them the riot act. One of the offending pilots, Captain Dolphin Overton, who had shot down two MiGs north of the border, was ordered stripped of his ace status, a punishment which was eventually rejected by higher authorities. Overton was never given official credit for the two kills north of the border. Flying with Overton at the time of his victories was his squadron commander, Colonel Edwin Heller, who was shot down 150 miles inside Manchuria. Heller was captured by the Chinese and mistreated, but was released after the war. January ended on a positive note, however, with 39 MiGs claimed for only two US losses. Two more American pilots also gained ace status.

In February the race to become the top ace of the war heated up. At that time the lead belonged to the late Major Davis with fourteen victories, but a new crop of MiG Killers was beginning to emerge. Rejoining the race was America's first jet ace, Major James Jabara, who had returned for another tour. In competition was Colonel Royal Baker with nine kills and two newcomers who were crowned that month: Captains Pete Fernandez and Joseph McConnell. Helping out in this race was the aggressive behavior of the MiG pilots who at times pushed far south to

Deck crewmen shovel snow off a tie down point on the flight deck of the USS ORISKANY (CV-34), amid F4U Corsairs and AD Skyraiders parked behind them. During the winter months, carrier operations off the Korean coast were extremely hazardous for both the pilots and the deck crews. Slippery conditions made it difficult when ser-vicing or rearming aircraft. Icy decks made landing conditions treacherous and created dangerous situations for deck crews — one slip could make them fall into a whirling propeller blade or overboard into the frigid water. (USN/NA)

Bombed up F4U-4N Corsairs line up in preparations for engine start aboard the ORISKANY, despite the waves crashing over the carrier's bow. Such conditions were a daily occurrence during the winter months in the Sea of Japan and the Yellow Sea. Flight operations were rarely canceled due to the weather. (USN/NA)

confront the Sabres. Large air battles took place with the enemy fighters coming out the losers. It was not all one-sided. On 7 April Captain Harold Fischer, an ace with ten kills, was shot down north of the border and captured. Five days later it was McConnell's turn to be downed by a MiG. McConnell was pulled from the Yellow Sea by an H-19 of the 3rd Air Sea Rescue Squadron. In general, the quality of the enemy pilots was inferior to that of their American counterparts, but as these enemy victories show, there was little room for complacency over 'MiG Alley.'

McConnell came back with a vengeance after being shot down. On 16 April he downed another MiG and, over the next month, shot down a further seven MiG-15s to end with a top score of sixteen. Pete Fernandez who ended up with fourteen and a half kills was close behind him. He was edged out of second place by Jabara who added nine more kills to his original score of six to finish with fifteen. It was rumored that McConnell was allowed to stay past his tour in order to achieve the top ranking ace status in preference to Fernandez due to his Latin ancestry. It was felt that McConnell made better copy than Fernandez and had more of the image of what an American fighter pilot should be. This has never been substantiated and in fact, higher authorities supposedly grounded Fernandez when they learned that the communists had placed a price on his head. The rumors didn't seem to bother McConnell or Fernandez; McConnell stood at Fernandez's side when he was married shortly after the war. Whatever the true story, both men carved a niche for themselves in the history of aerial warfare which will always reflect on their courage and ability.

Although the aerial battles up north continued with even greater feroc-ity, the communists had come back to the peace tables. During the last five months of the war, ten more pilots became jet aces, including one Marine, Major John Bolt, while on exchange duty with the 39th FS. There was one additional ace. Lt Guy Bordelon, flying an F4U-5N Corsair, was assigned to the USS PRINCETON, but was on detached duty to Pyontaek (K-6) to help stop nocturnal raids by enemy 'Bedcheck Charlies' against installations around Seoul. Most of these attacks used slow piston engine aircraft, which the faster F-94s and F3Ds were unable to engage. In three missions over a three week period of time Bordelon downed five aircraft, two each on 19 June and 1 July, and a single aircraft on 17 July to become the only Navy and only non-jet ace of the war.

By this stage of the war the experienced F-86 wings were operating in top form. Between March and July of 1953 (when the war ended) 225 MiGs were lost. In some cases the MiG pilots were so inexperienced that when a Sabre got behind them they ejected before they were fired upon. In other instances, MiG pilots lost control of their aircraft while dogfighting and spun in without the F-86 pilots having to take a shot. Others put their MiGs through such violent maneuvers that the tails separated from the fuselage. During this same period only ten F-86s were lost to enemy fighters, one of the best kill ratios ever achieved by American pilots. The last kill of the war occurred on 27 July, the last day of the war, when Captain Ralph Parr shot down a Russian Li-2 transport (a copy of the venerable C-47) which crossed over the Yalu into North Korea. The Russians claimed that Parr had shot the plane down over China and made plans to sue him in the World Court in The

Rolling seas can even toss around a large vessel such as a carrier. All the aircraft were tied down with steel cables to tie down points on the flight deck. In the middle of the deck is a F9F Panther in an experimental scheme of clear-coated natural metal. This coating was tried on different US Navy aircraft from April of 1952 until February of 1955 before it was discontinued due to corrosion problems. The Panthers are parked amid AD Skyraiders and F4U Corsairs. (USN/NA)

The lack of spare Sabre parts was an early problem, forcing many F-86s to be unavailable for operations. By 1953, the problem had been solved and the daily operational strength of the Sabre-equipped units was consistently high. This F-86E (52-2880) from the 334th FIS, 4th FIW has an engine change performed under snowy conditions at Kimpo. A special trailer was designed to hold the rear fuselage when it was unbolted from the forward section. Four hardened bolts held these two fuselage sections together. (USAF/NA)

Hague, but before it came to trial the Russians dropped the suit. A more serious form of retaliation by the Russians occurred two days after the incident. Russian MiG-15s shot down an RB-50 over international waters southeast of Vladivostok while it was on an electronic reconnaissance mission along the Russian coast. US analysts linked the two incidents together and felt the Soviets carried out the attack in direct response to the US attack. One crewman from the RB-50 was rescued by an American destroyer although it is believed some of the crew may have been captured by the Russians and kept for interrogation due to their specialized knowledge of radar and electronics.

Peace

Although the aerial battles over 'MiG Alley' captured headlines and made an impression on the communist high command, the bombing campaign was the primary means of bringing pressure on the North. The election of Dwight D. Eisenhower to the presidency, and the death of Josef Stalin, the Russian leader, laid the groundwork for a return to the truce talks. By April of 1953 there was guarded optimism that a breakthrough might be close at hand. There was also a Chinese attempt to seize more territory along the MLR in order to strengthen their bargaining position. In response to such moves the UN forces carried out hundreds of sorties daily in support of the ground troops. Inflammatory radio comments by the North Korean radio station in Pyongyang led to a massive strike against the facility after warning leaflets were dropped telling civilians to leave. On 1 May the station was leveled by wave

after wave of F-86s which lined up and dropped their bombs as if on a gunnery range. Despite the advance warning and the blatant attack on the North Korean capital, not one MiG tried to intercept the fighter-bombers, which were covered by higher flights of F-86s.

During May another series of attacks were carried out which helped get the peace talks back on track after the communist negotiators began to stall. Until this time the irrigation dams in North Korea had been off-limits — they were viewed as politically sensitive targets. Plans were drawn up to hit the Toksan, Chasan, and Kuwonga dams in western Korea using both Air Force and Marine aircraft. If the dams could be breached, the released water was expected to destroy crops and road and rail lines over an extensive area. On 13 May the Toksan dam was destroyed with extensive damage being done to both the rice crops and lines of communications. Chasan was next on 16 May — with similar results. The attack against the Kuwonga dam was not carried out until the night of 20 May. The delay allowed the North Koreans to lower the water level and negate the effects of the strike. Even so, the water loss severely affected the rice crop in the area and deprived the North Koreans of much needed food for the frontline troops. After these attacks negotiations picked up again, but the communists were still making probes along the MLR.

At the end of May the Chinese launched a series of attacks all along the MLR. The main attack came in early June when the Chinese hit the ROK II Corps around Kumsong. In response, the Air Force and Marines flew round-the-clock sorties using radar to guide them to targets at night or in the increasingly inclement weather. The Navy responded by keep-

Maintenance personnel wash down an F-86E (52-2846) from the 336th FIS, 4th FIW. Accumulated dirt and grime could slow an aircraft down and cause problems with controls and other moving parts. This Sabre wears the black and yellow ID bands introduced in 1952. These bands – applied to the outer wing surfaces and mid-fuselage – easily distinguished F-86s from similar-appearing MiG-15s in air combat. The yellow and black bands on the vertical stabilizer were unique to the 4th FIW. (USAF/NA)

A flight of F-86Es heads north looking for MiGs. FU-649 (50-649), *Aunt Myrna*, was flown by Lt Walter Copeland, who scored one victory in this aircraft. These Sabres were assigned to the 25th FIS, 51st FIW at Suwon (K-13). Aircraft of the 51st FIW wore black checks on the natural metal vertical stabilizers, with yellow and black ID bands on the wings and fuselages. (USAF/NA)

ing the carriers BOXER, PRINCETON, PHILIPPINE SEA, and LAKE CHAMPLAIN on line for seven days in support of the troops. The Chinese had hoped that the bad weather would help reduce air support for the UN ground forces, but the ground radar used to vector in attacking aircraft on targets laid waste to this hope. The critical day occurred on 15 June when the ROK troops began to give ground. On that day Air Force, Navy, and Marine aircrews flew 3,153 sorties — the largest number ever flown during the conflict. By 19 June the front had stabilized, but the Chinese were still not finished. On 13 July, the Chinese launched another series of attacks against the ROK troops and the US IX Corps on their flank. Again, massive aerial support saved the day and the enemy attack was blunted after severe fighting. This was to be the last major ground action of the war before the signing of the armistice.

While the final peace plans were readied for signing at Panmunjom, orders went out to make sure all airfields in North Korea were neutralized. This operation began in June, but by the end of the month bad weather had forced a halt to these attacks. On 19 July the UN Command sent out word of the impending armistice. The next day, an all-out series of day and night strikes were launched against the forty-three airfields used by the Chinese and North Koreans. At Uiju 21 MiGs were destroyed on the ground by B-29s and fighter-bombers. By the time the armistice took effect on 27 July every airfield in North Korea was unser-

viceable for jet aircraft. While the clock ticked down toward the last minutes of the war the last missions of the war were being flown by night flying B-26s which destroyed a number of trucks and carried out radar-directed close support missions. Just before 2201 hours when the armistice went into effect, a lone RB-26 from the 67th Tactical Reconnaissance Wing crossed back into South Korea completing the last official mission of the long conflict. The war was finally over.

Aftermath

Although the official end of the fighting occurred on the night of 27 July 1953, Korea today is still a divided country; men continue to fight and die along the frontline. Despite the huge outlay of lives and material, the border between the two countries is almost identical to what it was back in June of 1950. Yet the Korean War was a turning point in the Cold War. Despite the costs, the United States and the United Nations stood firm against naked communist aggression in Korea. Stalin came to realize that, when confronted, the US was a dangerous enemy and one not to be lightly regarded. New data coming out of Russia suggests that if there had not been a stand in Korea, there would have been more confrontations, which would have led to World War Three. This alone may be the ultimate legacy of the war.

There are many loose ends, which still exist from the war. Many of

The pilot of this MiG-15 was caught ejecting from his fighter by the gun camera of an F-86 flown by Lt Edwin 'Buzz' Aldrin. He was given credit for this 'kill' — one of two Aldrin achieved while flying with the 16th FIS, 51st FIW. Aldrin would later become an astronaut and walk on the Moon during the Apollo 11 mission in July of 1969. During the course of 1953, it became open season on the MiGs since most of the pilots sent up against the Sabres were totally inexperienced. Occasionally, Sabre pilots would run into some 'honchos' (veteran pilots), like the ones who downed aces Joe McConnell and Harold Fischer. (USAF/NA)

LT-6Gs prepare to take off on a FAC mission in early 1953. There was always the danger the communists would try to escalate the war with a surprise attack against UN airbases — sandbagged revetments were built to provide protection for individual aircraft. Although no major attacks ever occurred, the communists made many attacks against airfields and other installations using old trainers and other prop-driven aircraft, usually at night. Sometimes known as 'Bedcheck Charlies,' these raiders – often flying Polikarpov Po-2 biplanes – proved to be a major nuisance. (USAF/NA)

the pilots who were captured were never accounted for and it is believed that a significant number of these were transported to the Soviet Union for interrogation. This has been confirmed by recent documents unearthed and released by the current Russian government. In particular F-86 pilots were singled out along with bomber crewmen with knowledge of radar and electronics. Whatever became of these men can only be guessed — and it is highly unlikely that any of these missing men are still alive somewhere in Russia.

It has also been confirmed that Russian and Eastern European pilots flew hundreds of combat missions against American and UN pilots along the Yalu throughout the war. The Russians rotated units in order to give them combat experience much like they had done during the Spanish Civil War. There had been numerous claims by American pilots throughout the war that they had flown against non-Asian pilots and intelligence also suspected this. However, this was kept quiet by US officials in order not to provoke the American public. There was some fear that there would be a call to expand the war against the Soviet Union. The MiG-15 attack against the Panthers off the ORISKANY cited earlier lends credence to this view.

In line with this a close examination of Russian records show that there were five Soviet aces from World War Two who participated in the fighting and became aces again. Russian accounts credit forty-four

of their pilots with five or more victories. Their top ranking aces were Captain Nikolay Sutiagin, with twenty-one victories, and Colonel Evgeniy Pepelyaev with twenty kills. If these records are accurate these two pilots were the top aces of the conflict, beating the top American ace Captain Joseph McConnell for this honor. While some historians may question these Russian claims, it need only be remembered that a number of American aces were shot down including McConnell and George Davis. This does lend support to the Russian claims, but there is still considerable room for further examination of such records to gain a clearer view of the actual scope of Russian victory claims.

American pilots noted at times the MiG pilots were both extremely aggressive and skillful and were nicknamed 'Honchos' by their counterparts in recognition of their ability. What these records do serve to highlight is that the battles which were fought over 'MiG Alley' were not so one-sided as some writers would have the public believe. This serves to enhance the accomplishments achieved by the American F-86 pilots who took on a numerically superior foe while operating at the limits of their range and under political restrictions. There is an old Arab saying, "The courage of your enemy does you justice." In the savage aerial battles over the Yalu this quote is most appropriate to the airmen of both sides.

UN forces tried different ways to stop these night intruders, including Lockheed F-94 Starfires – the most sophisticated night-fighter in the US inventory. This F-94B (50-869) from the 319th FIS is being towed back to its revetment at Suwon following a night mission over the Seoul/Kimpo area in June of 1953. The two blue stripes on the aft fuselage indicated this Starfire was a flight leader's aircraft. The 39th FIS emblem appeared under the cockpit, while the tail stripe was red. (USAF/NA)

An F-94B (51-5416) brightens the ramp with its afterburner during a full power run-up prior to takeoff from Suwon in the early summer of 1953. Two F-94s were lost during the war: one stalled out when it lowered its airspeed to keep pace with a Po-2 biplane, and another collided with an enemy aircraft during an interception. (USAF/NA)

A ground crewman pumps hot air into the engine intake of SUNNY, an F-86E (52-2887) from the 51st FIW. The heated air warmed up the oil and hydraulic fluids before the General Electric J47 engine was started. This type of ground support was necessary if the jets were to be able to operate in the cold weather, which often fell below 0° Fahrenheit (-18° Celsius). Another mechanic is peering into the F-86's cockpit, while two others stand on the Sabre's wing tending to the mid-fuselage area. A ground power unit plugged into the aircraft's mid-fuselage provided the electrical power for starting the engine. (USAF/NA)

The pilot of F-86F *Patricia* (52-4777) gives the 'thumbs up' sign to his crew chief while his engine kicks over with the assist of the starter cart. The insignia on the fuselage side is a variation of the standard 'boxing pigeon' emblem used by the 334th FIS, 4th FIW. (USAF/NA)

While the F-86s wreaked havoc on the MiGs, the fighter-bombers carried out their daily routine against ground targets. This F-84G takes off from Taegu in search of enemy road traffic north of the Main Line of Resistance (MLR), and is armed with two 1000 lb (453.6 KG) bombs under the wings. The Thunderjet was assigned to the 49th FBW at Kunsan (K-8). (USAF/NA)

The fighter-bombers caused tremendous damage to enemy troops, vehicles, and supplies. Repeated strikes by US Navy Panthers have created huge columns of smoke in front of this F9F making an attack run with four napalm containers under the wings. Napalm – an incendiary material composed of naphtha and palm oil – was a favorite weapon against most targets except bridges, rail lines, roads, and dams. (USN/NA)

One of the most prodigious of bomb haulers was the Navy's AD Skyraider, which could carry a heavier payload than a World War II B-17 Flying Fortress. The deck crew prepares this AD-4 for a mission from the USS BOXER while the pilot makes his pre-flight walk around. Two 500 lb (226.8 KG) general purpose bombs and three 250 lb (113.4 KG) fragmentation bombs are mounted on the underwing racks of the folded starboard wing. The Douglas Skyraider would later see service in Vietnam where the USAF was forced to swallow its pride and use this Navy aircraft in the ground support role since it had nothing comparable in its own inventory. (USN/NA)

Constant surveillance of enemy airfields and supply lines was essential in order to prevent the communists from building up their forces. An F2H-2P (PP-33) from VC-61 has just returned from a mission along the Yalu to check out enemy airfields. This variant of the Banshee featured an elongated nose section housing cameras. A VF-11 F2H-2 (T-114) flew along as an escort due to the threat of MiGs. These aircraft are flying above their home carrier, the USS KEARSARGE. Mission tallies were painted under the canopies of the two Banshees. (USN/NA)

A natural metal F9F-5 of VF-111 comes in for a landing aboard the USS BOXER. This scheme was tried on a few aircraft in different units to see how well it reacted to salt water. Some aircraft were painted half Glossy Sea Blue to compare the painted and clear-coated natural metal surfaces. The natural metal scheme was not adopted due to corrosion problems. The overall Glossy Sea Blue color scheme was replaced with the Light Gull Gray over Gloss White finish beginning on 23 February 1955. (USN/NA)

By the spring of 1953, the ace race was in full stride. The leader was Captain Manuel J. 'Pete' Fernandez, who flew a number of F-86s, including this Sabre normally assigned to Capt R. T. Dewey. Fernandez was assigned to the 334th FIS, 4th FIW at Kimpo (K-14). The G-suit worn over his flight suit prevented blood from pooling below the waist during high-G (force of gravity) maneuvers and preventing the pilot from 'blacking out.' Fernandez and other US fighter pilots were normally issued G-suits. (USAF/NA)

One of Fernandez's kills goes down over 'MiG Alley.' The MiG-15 appears to be camouflaged in shades of green and brown. Many of these fighters were delivered to the war zone in natural metal. Fernandez ended the war with 14.5 victories – the third-highest 'kill' total for US pilots in the Korean War. (USAF/NA)

Fernandez is congratulated on one of his kills by Major James Jabara (left), the first ace of the Korean War. On 20 May 1951, Jabara downed two aircraft to raise his score to six 'kills.' He returned to the 334th FIS for a second tour of duty and eventually edged out Fernandez with 15 kills. (USAF/NA)

Captains Joseph McConnell (left) and Manuel Fernandez participate in a news conference in Washington, DC to discuss the battles over 'MiG Alley.' McConnell, of the 39th FIS, 51st FIW, claimed the honor for top US ace of the Korean War with 16 MiG-15s shot down. Both

McConnell and Fernandez were grounded and ordered home to prevent a repetition of what happened to Major George Davis, who was killed in action in 1952. (USAF/NA)

Leading US Air Force Aces

Pilot	Victories
Capt Joseph McConnell	16
Maj James Jabara	15
Capt Manuel J. 'Pete' Fernandez, Jr.	14.5
Maj George A. Davis	14
Maj Frederick C. 'Boots' Blesse	10
Capt Ralph S. Parr	10
Lt Col Vermont Garrison	10
Capt Harold E. Fischer	10
Col James K. Johnson	10
Capt Lonnie R. Moore	10

Leading Russian Aces

Pilot	Victories
Capt Nikolay Sutiagin	21
Col Evgeniy Pepelyaev	20
Lt Col Aleksander Smorzkov	15
Capt Lew Szczukin	15
Capt Serafin Subbotin	15
Maj Dimitri Oskin	14
Capt Mikhail Ponomariev	14
Capt Sergei Kramarenko	13

The war ended with the signing of an armistice at Panmunjom on 27 July 1953. This VF-194 AD-4Q Skyraider was one of the last aircraft lost in the conflict. It suffered an engine failure on launch from the USS BOXER (CV-21) and crashed into the sea. The pilot is climbing out of the cockpit, apparently unhurt. The fin tip and rudder trim tab stripes were Light Yellow (FS14187). (USN/NA)

Crewmen aboard the BOXER hear the news that the war is over from their Captain, yet are unusually low-keyed about it. With the many earlier rumors of the war ending, GIs were more than a little skeptical that the communists would actually keep the peace. The sailors are gathered near an F2H-2P Banshee and an F9F Panther. (USN/NA)

These Air Force pilots are much more demonstrative in their feelings about the end of the war. They have just completed a 'Peace Patrol' in case the communists were planning to launch a surprise attack. Firing his pistol into the air is Major Foster Smith, who had four and a half kills. Climbing out of the 335th FIS F-86 is Captain Clyde Curtin, who scored five victories. On the right is Captain Ralph Parr who claimed the last kill of the war, a Soviet Il-12 transport for which the Soviets tried to sue him in the World Court. Parr's victory was his tenth, which tied him for sixth-best among US pilots in the conflict. (USAF/NA)

Despite the end of the war, the uneasy truce which followed did not allow the UN forces to drop their guard. This F-86F from the 336th FIS, 4th FIW is refueled in late 1953. The Wing marking on the tail band is a post-Korean War practice. Aircraft were kept fully fueled in order to be ready for a quick takeoff in case of possible enemy attack and to prevent condensation buildup caused by extremes in temperature. (USAF/NA)

(Above) Three years after the truce was signed, the 58th FBG at Osan was still flying missions over Korea. KATHY'S KALAMITIZER (52-4829) wears the unit's new markings – red nose and tail bands, white stars, and black lightning bolts and trim. The F-86F still carries the black-trimmed yellow fuselage identification band associated with the Korean War. The pilot steps into the Sabre's cockpit with his crew chief ready to assist him. (USAF/NA)

(Below) The South Korean Air Force began to receive F-86s after the war ended. Aside from the markings – a variation of the US national insignia – these F-86Fs sitting in revetments could pass for USAF Sabres, which had sat there a few years earlier. Newer jets now patrol above the Korean peninsula — still considered one of the most dangerous points for a possible outbreak of hostilities — 50 years after the truce was signed. (USAF/NA)